FOOLES AND FRICASSEES:
FOOD IN SHAKESPEARE'S ENGLAND

FOOLES AND FRICASSEES:
FOOD IN SHAKESPEARE'S ENGLAND

Edited by
Mary Anne Caton

With an Essay by
Joan Thirsk

The Folger Shakespeare Library
Washington, D. C., 1999

Distributed by University of Washington Press
Seattle and London

This volume has been published in conjunction
with the exhibition *Fooles and Fricassees: Food in
Shakespeare's England,* presented from September 10 through
December 30, 1999, at the Folger Shakespeare Library,®
Washington, D.C.

Werner Gundersheimer, Director.

The exhibition and the catalogue were funded by
The Winton and Carolyn Blount Exhibitions Endowment
and The Andrew W. Mellon Publications Fund of the
Folger Library.

Photographs by Julie Ainsworth.

Editorial and Production Coordinator:
Rachel Doggett, Andrew W. Mellon Curator of Books.

Distributed by University of Washington Press,
Seattle and London.
ISBN 0-295-97926-7

Design: Studio A, Alexandria, Virginia.
Printing: Hagerstown Bookbinding and Printing,
Hagerstown, Maryland.

Cover: Watercolor miniature (English, early seventeenth
century), from a collection of royal, military, and court
costumes of the time of James I.

Frontispiece: Etching by Wenceslaus Hollar from
The fables of Aesop, paraphras'd in verse…the 2d ed.
By John Ogilby. London, 1668.

TABLE OF CONTENTS

Today, when foods from almost every part of the world are readily available in our supermarkets, it seems natural to assume that the diet of Shakespeare and his contemporaries—made up primarily of what could be gathered or caught in local fields, hedgerows, and forests—was limited and rather dull. As Joan Thirsk demonstrates, however, sixteenth-century Englishmen were familiar with a wide range of foodstuffs and seasonings and had strong opinions about the flavor and quality of what they ate. It is Dr. Thirsk's research on the agricultural history of England and the numerous bits of information about people's diets she has found in surviving documents that inspired this exhibition. *Fooles and Fricassees* follows and complements two other exhibitions, *Elizabethan Households* (1995) and *The Housewife's Rich Cabinet* (1997), that have explored how English men and women of the sixteenth and seventeenth centuries lived and provided for themselves.

The domestic world of those who prepared the daily bread and ale consumed by Shakespeare's countrymen is revealed most vividly in the manuscript "receipt books" they have left us. There we find recipes for "pease pottage," a staple of the average person's diet, for "stew[ing] a calves head," or making a "gooseberry foole," recorded in the hands of the women (and men) who prepared these dishes three or four hundred years ago. Sarah Longe compiled her *Receipt Booke* about 1610. She was, says Heidi Brayman Hackel, "one of the respectable middling sort, the wife perhaps of a successful tradesman or a member of the lesser gentry." She recorded a recipe for biscuits that were enjoyed by King James and his Queen, but it is another biscuit recipe in her book that reveals the vast differences between

her kitchen and ours. "Take halfe a pound of sugar, as much flower," she begins. Then, after adding eleven eggs and a few spoonfuls of rose-water: "Beate it 2 hours. . .; bake it an hour. . .; then you must dry it againe in the Sun or Oven." Another recipe for a cake begins, "Take halfe a bushell of fflower, 8 pound of Currence, and 5 pound of butter. . . ." Feeding her family and entertaining guests were formidable tasks for Sarah Longe, even with servants to assist her. Her *Receipt Booke*, transcribed in full in Appendix I, is one of many such books in the Folger collection that illustrate the variety to be found in the food consumed in early modern England.

The Folger Library is very grateful to Joan Thirsk for serving as advisor to the exhibition and for providing a delightful overview of "Food in Shakespeare's England" for this catalogue. Until her retirement, Dr. Thirsk was Reader in Economic History at the University of Oxford and Professorial Fellow of St. Hilda's College. She is the General Editor of the multi-volume *Agrarian History of England and Wales* and the author of a number of other works, including *Economic Policy and Projects: The Development of a Consumer Society* (1978), *England's Agricultural Regions and Agrarian History, 1500–1750* (1987), and *Alternative Agriculture, a History from the Black Death to the Present Day* (1997).

Mary Anne Caton, formerly Curator of Agecroft Association in Richmond and now Curator of Fraunces Tavern Museum in New York City, participated in a 1997 Folger Institute seminar on the subject of "Food History and Food Theories, 1500–1700," directed by Joan Thirsk. When I asked Mary Anne if she would be interested in curating an exhibition on the subject of food, she readily agreed to do so. She has assembled a fascinating array of manuscript and printed materials documenting not only what people ate but where the food came from, how it was grown, preserved, seasoned, and served, and what people believed about various foods' benefits to their health. She has also prevailed upon colleagues at other institutions to lend us a few of the objects that would have been used to prepare and serve some of the recipes on display. Our thanks go to Agecroft Association, the Jamestown-Yorktown Foundation, the New-York Historical Society, Pilgrim Hall, and Plimoth Plantation. In addition, we wish to thank Mr. George Way and Mr. Jonathan Z. Friedman for lending objects from their personal collections.

Rosalind Larry, Assistant Reading Room Supervisor at the Folger Library, and Camille Seerattan, Reference Assistant, assisted Mary Anne Caton in finding collection materials for the exhibition and in translating some of them. Ronald W. Fuchs, Curatorial Assistant at Winterthur, helped with catalogue entries, and Heidi Brayman Hackel of Oregon State University provided an introduction to the *Receipt Booke* of Sarah Longe. My thanks go to E. Dever Powell for his help with the transcription of the Longe manuscript. Others who assisted with the exhibition are acknowledged in Mary Anne Caton's Introduction.

From books on herbs and medicine, and laws governing the baking of bread and the importing of pepper, from household accounts, gardening journals, and even student plays— as well as recipe books—the curator of the exhibition and her assistants have garnered a remarkable amount of information about food in Shakespeare's England. We hope that you will enjoy the glimpse that these materials provide into the gardens, kitchens, butteries, and cellars of the past and of the food grown, prepared and stored there.

Rachel Doggett
Andrew W. Mellon Curator of Books

August hath .31. dayes:

Dame Ceres now the empty barnes ✶ with store of ripened fruites doth fill ✶
O happy waight, that grace obtaines ✶ And strength from god, so do his will

Day houre	breaketh minut	Sonne houre	ryseth minut	Sunne houre	setteth minut	The twylight houre	minut
.2	.10.	.4	.37.	.7	.23.	.9	.80.

The day is .14. houres and .46. minutes. The night is .9. houres and .14. minutes

As burning heate will thee destroy ✶ So shiueryng colde will thee anoy ✶ ss
Let lytle sleepe thee now content ✶ Purge not, nor bleed, lest thou repent ✶ ss

INTRODUCTION

"For Profit and Pleasure":
Changes in Food and Farming
by Mary Anne Caton

This exhibition grew out of the 1997 Folger Institute seminar "Food History and Food Theories, 1500–1700," directed by Professor Joan Thirsk. Professor Thirsk's work on agricultural history together with her own practical experience as a cook had made her question some assumptions about the diets and foods available in early modern England. What biases had caused many historians to dismiss early food as flavorless and monotonous? What could be learned from a more careful approach to this inquiry, and what information exists about everyday foods? What could sixteenth-century school texts teach us about the flavor of bread or preferences for flours? Recent annotated editions of manuscript recipes by Elinor Fettiplace (c1604) and of the Martha Washington family manuscript (c1600) have begun to fill a gap that exists between food historians of the academy and those who work in the kitchen. Each group has much to learn from the other. This catalogue addresses themes of interest to both sorts of food historians while following the organization of the exhibition. Section titles from the exhibition serve as subheadings within the text that documents the books, manuscripts, and three-dimensional objects displayed.

The exhibition addresses food in its broadest sense, from its origins in traditional and alternative crops through agricultural innovation, transportation to market, and household provisioning to its appearance on the table in old and new foods and beverages. Each section presents materials to illustrate one aspect of the relationship between dietary change and social transformation. The first four sections present basic information about diet and medicine in early modern England. Manuals on health explain the fundamental relationship that was understood to exist between food and medicine. Each ingredient in a prepared dish was believed to affect the humors of the person eating it. Ill health was thought to come from an imbalance in one's humors and was treated with appropriate medicines produced by either an apothecary or a housewife. According to the doctrines of the Greek physician Galen, the four humors that characterized each plant, animal, and human were choler, phlegm, melancholy, and blood. The way to health was a balanced body; that balance was modified by the composition of one's diet, for each food had a humor, or character, that defined its proper medicinal and culinary uses. Thus, recipes for medical treatments appear alongside those for table-top dishes in many of the collections of recipes included in the exhibition. So too do recipes for preserving since it was the housewife who doctored her family and servants with stillroom waters and medicines made from garden and orchard plants, spices, and other ingredients.

Bread and ale and pottage formed the basic daily diet for most of the population. Tastes in breads and flours varied from one area of the country to another and, often, according to one's occupation. Fruit infusions recommended for the poor by Thomas Tryon in his *A new art of brewing* (1691) show how one type of readily available food could provide nutritious beverages. Printed Lenten menus often reveal what dairy products and vegetable dishes supplemented the basic bread and pottage. Spices were used to create the pungent/sweet palate found in most cooking.

Opposite: Illustration for the month of August, from Thomas Trevelyon's Pictorial commonplace book (Manuscript, 1608).

Originally Arabian, these flavors were brought to Europe by returning Crusaders in the thirteenth century. English cuisine combined the flavors of imported spices like cinnamon, nutmeg, pepper, and cloves with herbs and acidic binders or liaisons like verjuice (liquid from pressed unripe apples or grapes) or vinegar. Spices were imported from the Spice Islands in Malaysia by Portuguese and Venetian merchants. Foreign grocery imported into London in 1559 included highly-valued amounts of cinnamon, sugar, and French wines, as well as currants, dates, figs, ginger, marmalade, nutmeg, and pepper. Luxuries like sugar first appeared in western cookery as medicines, and sugar was valued for its supposed health benefits into the eighteenth century. (Wheaton, 19) The sweet, spicy cuisine that characterized medieval European food was slowly replaced by one of salty and acidic flavors.

The center sections of the exhibition explore foreign influences and specific areas of farming where imported plants and techniques changed English agricultural habits. Imported luxury foods new in 1550 had by 1675 become more widespread, in part because of published accounts and manuals. Hot liquids—chocolate, tea, and coffee—began to change how the elite socialized after 1650. Hot drinks were initially considered medicines, and as they became popular pleasures, excessive consumption sparked fierce debates about the effects of over-indulgence. At the same time that England was importing new products it was increasing its exports. The emerging market for English products in the sixteenth century included dairy produce such as milk and butter as well as the more familiar bales of cloth. Between Michelmas 1662 and Michelmas 1663, over 21,000 firkins of butter valued at more than £18,000 and 378 cwt. of cheeses valued at £460 were exported from London. Agricultural crops like hops, linseed, rapecakes, starch, and woad were exported in smaller quantities, and small amounts of molasses and refined sugar were exported as well. Like dairy produce, some beverages (aqua vitae, beer, and strong waters) went out in large shipments. These exports are a frac-

tion of England's total exports. (Thirsk, 186–188) Concern for England's economic health is evident in discussions about reliance on foreign products. Projects for improving English agriculture frequently discuss alternative crops like saffron, as John Worlidge does in *Systema Agriculturae* (1699). Alternative crops—grasses (livestock fodder), hops (for brewing), saffron—offered farmers ways to profit and diversify production. Improved plow blades, increased manuring, reclamation of fen lands, foreign gardeners and the plants they brought with them, and attention to new manuals published in English all contributed to a climate of agricultural improvement.

One major change for the upper classes during the seventeenth century was the addition of more fresh vegetables and fruits to their diets. Publications describing new discoveries led English gardeners and farmers to experiment with what William Harrison called "roots from Spain, Portingale, and the Indies." (Harrison, 129) New root crops like carrots and turnips were being grown for table consumption. (Kerridge, 268–269) William Lawson's *A new orchard and garden* (1618) and similar gardening manuals advise proper care for such exotic plants as asparagus, strawberries, and melons. Flavors changed from the medieval sweet/spicy palate to the acidic/salty one familiar to modern diners, as in the salad almanac in John Evelyn's *Acetaria* (1699). The numerous fruit preserves and conserves found in Sarah Longe's recipe book (c1610) attest to the growing availability of damsons, cherries, quinces, apricots, raspberries, and gooseberries. A transcription of Longe's recipes begins on page 102.

The mechanics of provisioning an early modern household include marketing and methods of food preparation. Hugh Alley's sketches of London markets made in 1598 show farmers and herbwives from Essex, Kent, Surrey, Middlesex, and London, each selling particular provisions. The account book maintained for a London household from 1612 to 1614 records what the steward paid to provision the family's buttery, cellar, and pantry. Although Thomas Betts (d. 1658) left an estate with few fancy goods worth only seventy-eight pounds, we can guess that his dinners comprised boiled stuffs (from his kettle), roasted meats and fowl (from his spit), and complex dishes simmered in his two skillets. Susanna Packe's recipe for salted eels, one of many preserving recipes in printed and manuscript cookery books, shows how foods were preserved to last through the winter. French influence is found in numerous recipes such as Mary Hookes's boiled capon in white sauce which has a French binder or roûx made of flour. Particularly influential was La Varenne's *The French Cook*, translated for English audiences.

We learn something about the social significance of food from works that address manners for both diners and servants. Proper instruction in table manners and in how to serve a meal became a popular topic for instructional manuals in the 1600s. Hannah Woolley's guides, for example, provide rules for the housewife's many roles—as steward, hostess, guest, and employer—with etiquette spelled out for "ladies, gentlewomen, and maids." Elaborate carving instructions for joints of meat as well as for unusual vegetables like artichokes remind us that the presentation of food formed a ritualized entertainment, of which banqueting "stuffe" (sugar plate, marmalade) was a part. Henry Butts's collection of table talk presents basic cultivation and cooking facts about joints and pies while Robert Speed's view of dining in company introduces a rowdier bunch of companions who clearly have dispensed with conversational niceties. The exhibition concludes with a look at Christmas foods and hospitality as they are presented in two seventeenth-century plays featuring characters such as Queen Mince Pie. *A Christmas messe* (a single portion of food), performed at an Oxford or Cambridge college about 1600, concerns the battle between King Brawn and King Beef over who is served first. Robert Plot recalls Christmas hospitality in Staffordshire about 1660 that included indulgence in plentiful foods during the twelve days of celebrations. This feasting, associated with the beginning of winter, reminded celebrants of the lean months ahead, when fresh meats, cheeses, vegetables for pottage, and herbs would be difficult to find.

Many people have provided help and encouragement during this project. The ever-gracious Folger staff patiently answered long-distance questions and scanned materials for me. I particularly want to thank Rachel Doggett, Andrew W. Mellon Curator of Books, for her precise nurturing of the project as a companion to earlier exhibitions on housewifery and Elizabethan households. I also want to thank Betsy Walsh, Reading Room Supervisor, Laetitia Yeandle, Curator of Manuscripts, and Reading Room staff members Rosalind Larry, Camille Seerattan, Sulyn Taylor, and LuEllen DeHaven. J. Franklin Mowery, Head of Conservation, with Linda Blaser, Julie Biggs, and Linda Hohneke prepared and mounted the objects on display. Julie Ainsworth photographed materials for the catalogue.

Curators and staff of other institutions generously supported the project with many kindnesses. Special thanks to Agecroft Association, the Jamestown-Yorktown Foundation, the New-York Historical Society, Pilgrim Hall, and Plimoth Plantation. At Agecroft, Deborah de Arechega, Susan Bradbrooke, Sandi Barnette, Laura Carr, Sandy Jensen, Alice Young, and interns Cheryl Denbar, Suzi Magill, and Lee McAllister; at the Jamestown-Yorktown Foundation, Thomas C. Davidson and Mark Cattanach; at the New-York Historical Society, Margi Hofer, Jack Rutland, and Kim Terbusch; at Pilgrim Hall and Plimoth Plantation, Karin Goldstein. George Way's generosity and knowledge of early modern objects make him an inspiring neighbor. Colleagues in Professor Thirsk's seminar, as well as Heidi Brayman Hackel, Ronald W. Fuchs II, Juana Green, Jessie McNab, and Barbara Wheaton, discussed issues relating to foodways and material culture. Finally, Kevin Murphy's inspiration and generous support made this work an exciting intellectual adventure. His help encouraged me to think clearly. I dedicate this book to him for all these reasons, and for all those that remain personal.

Ther is much feasting in this moneth but few the better for it

FOOD IN SHAKESPEARE'S ENGLAND

Dr. Joan Thirsk
University of Oxford

Food has been so much taken for granted that few people in the past have left us clear accounts to enlighten us about their customs. Moreover, small changes in diet have been continual and are therefore difficult to identify from one generation to the next. Subtle shifts of emphasis often affect small groups only, whether communities in distinct localities or single classes, and they make no stir in the wider world. Diet and dietary changes in Shakespeare's England, however, can be determined more clearly than for preceding generations. More and more books were being printed at this time, and as food is a subject of never-failing interest, references to it began to appear in literature discussing medicine and health. Authors advanced a variety of food theories and in passing remarks revealed something of the food that was eaten at the time, the way it was cooked, and differences in diet among classes.

People were also traveling further afield than hitherto; more of them traveled in Europe, some went to the Far East, and others ventured across the Atlantic. They encountered new foodstuffs that at first seemed strange and then became acceptable. Their accounts stimulated more interest in the discussion of food, and botanists and university scholars added their voices to those of the travelers and the medical men. Thus we get glimpses of many conflicting opinions on what should and should not be eaten, of what was in fashion, and of the different tastes introduced by foreigners living in England. Some people compiled cookbooks in manuscript for their own use, and in time cookbooks began to appear in print. Reading all these texts four centuries later, we learn something of the general food habits and the enthusiasms and prejudices of Shakespeare's day. We can detect, as well, some of the basic assumptions of the time—enough to check our inclination to impose our own values and tastes, anachronistically, on the past.

DIET

It is conventional to describe the diet of ordinary people in the sixteenth century as dull and monotonous, dominated by cereals, beans, and peas, and constrained by the rules about fasting that obliged people to eat fish, or at least refrain from meat, on nearly half the days in the year—on two days a week before 1550, on three days a week after 1563, and always in Lent.[1] In fact, ordinary folk in Shakespeare's day, as long as they had a roof over their heads and a kitchen fire, were able to eat foods of great variety without spending much money. The changing seasons gave them greens, roots, herbs, fruits, and nuts, many of which could be gathered in nearby hedgerows, fields, and woods, or plucked from their own gardens. In all these places there were innumerable plants and flowers for stews and salads. People appreciated the varied flavors of bread made with different cereals, whether wheat, barley, rye, or oats, or a mixture of these. They ate every part of the animals that came their way: eyes, snouts, brains, lungs, and feet, the noses, lips, and palates of calves and steers, ox cheeks, the udders and tongues of young cattle, and lambs' stones. Gentlemen welcomed the entrails of deer brought and sold to them at the back door of the manor house. They ate

Opposite: A December dinner, from Thomas Fella, *A book of diverse devices* (Manuscript, 1585–1598, 1622).

every bird in the sky: bustards, herons, heath-cocks, bitterns, gulls, peewits, pigeons, larks, robins, and sparrows. Rooks (crows) were left for the poor, but fieldfares (thrushes) were positively savored by gourmets at harvest time, for then they had fattened themselves on ripe juniper berries that gave their meat a special flavor. All fish were eaten as well, whether large or small, from freshwater rivers or from the sea.[2]

People of Shakespeare's day had strong opinions about the flavor and quality of meat. They used clever tricks to breed or trap birds and kept the wild ones in cages for a week or two to fatten them. The birds were fed pennyroyal, rosemary, and other aromatic herbs to flavor their meat. Capons were crammed with barley, wheatmeal bran, and warm ale or beer, or, if economy dictated, were given seeds of cockle (Lychnis) and leaves and seeds of melilot (a sweet clover). All birds were considered more flavorful if they were caught in flight. The flavor of beef from oxen that had worked at the plow was believed to be superior to that of grazing cattle. Mutton from sheep fed on peas in winter was not as good as mutton fed on grass, and that fed on short grass tasted better than that fed on the coarser grass of enclosures. Pork from pigs that ate grass and nuts in the woods was infinitely better than pork from pigs fed kitchen waste or, even worse, the industrial waste of town industries such as starchhouses.[3]

In short, sixteenth-century Englishmen were familiar with a far larger range of foodstuffs procured locally than we are today, and they were sensitive to subtly different flavors. Over the centuries our economy has encouraged production on an ever larger scale and has gradually reduced the number of home-produced, edible foods available while encouraging the importing of more exotic goods from abroad. In Shakespeare's day, in contrast, a high proportion of the population lived in the countryside, had access to wild plants, animals, and birds in the fields and woods, and ate mostly the foods produced in their own locality. Diets were biased toward local specialties, varied regionally, and

included a great many foods that are now totally unfamiliar, some of them to our loss.

Regional differences are amply illustrated in surviving documents. The household accounts of the Reynell family of Forde in Devon show them regularly consuming pilchards in great quantity. This fish is plentiful off the Devon and Cornwall coasts, whereas large numbers of eels were available to be eaten in the East Anglian fens.[4] Keepers of parks consumed venison "all the time," wrote Thomas Moffett, a physician in Elizabeth's reign, noting that children fed on it were very healthy. Near Brighton, in East Sussex, the warren at Albourne Chase was said to produce 100,000 rabbits a year, and Moffett took it for granted that rabbit meat was common fare for many local people.[5]

Today we cannot differentiate regionally the numerous varieties of herbs that were available, but we do know their great number and varied uses. James I's physician, Theodore Mayerne, commended innumerable herbs to his patients. His papers show that he urged nursing women to eat a daily diet that included succory (chicory), lettuce, sorrel, purslane, plantain, borage, bugloss, thyme, and vervain.[6] Not one of these plants was exotic. Investigating purslane alone we find that it was extremely common in salads and that there were recipes for pickling it to be ready to eat in two weeks. It was much valued in winter. Mayerne's notes of advice to nursing women also include his recommendation of another assortment of common herbs: dill, fennel and fennel seed, rocket, smallage (a variety of celery or parsley), and a decoction of coleworts (cabbages).[7]

MEAT AND POTTAGE

Meat was considered the most desirable food in the sixteenth century. Foreigners saw so much of it in the towns and in the houses of the well-to-do that they always commented on the large amount of meat eaten by the English. Printed menus of the time are always those of the upper classes and certainly show many meat dishes at every meal. Even the rich, however, did not necessarily

12. A Dish of souced Fish.
13. A Dish of pickled Oysters.
14. A Dish of Anchovies and Caveare.

A Bill of Fare without Feasting; only such a number of Dishes as are used in Great and Noble Houses for their own Family, and for familiar Friends with them.

The First Course in Summer Season.

1. A Fine Pudding boiled or baked.
2. A Dish of boiled Chickens.
3. Two Carps stewed or a boiled Pike.
4. A Florentine in Puff-paste.
5. A Calves Head, the one half hashed, and the other boiled.
6. A Haunch of Venison rosted.
7. A Venison Pasty.
8. A Couple of fat Capons, or a Pig, or both.

The

The Second Course.

1. A Dish of Partridges.
2. An Artichoke Pie.
3. A Dish of Quails.
4. A cold Pigeon Pie.
5. A Souced Pig.
6. A Joll of fresh Salmon.
7. A Dish of Tarts of several sorts.
8. A *Westphalia* Gammon, and dryed Tongues about it.

A Bill of Fare in Winter in Great Houses.

1. A Collar of Brawn.
2. A Capon and White Broth, or two boiled Rabbits.
3. Two rosted Neats Tongues and an Udder between them.
4. A Chine of Beef rosted.
5. A made Dish in Puff-paste.
6. A Shoulder of Mutton stuffed with Oysters.

7. A

One of several sample bills of fare provided by Hannah Woolley in *The Queen-like Closet* (London, 1675).

eat massive amounts of meat at a sitting. Rather, they tasted several kinds in small quantities, knowing that the food left uneaten at the high table would be passed to the lower ranks of servants in the household and would finally reach the poor waiting at the gate. James I, for example, is reported to have taken small portions from eight to ten delicate dishes, and since he ate little or no bread, he probably consumed only a moderate quantity of food. Those of more modest means relied on a meat bone with fragments of meat attached or a small slice of bacon, which they cut from a flitch hanging in the rafters, to flavor a stew. A yeoman farmer living near Southport, Lancashire, at a later date (1724–1767) frequently bought a sheep's head.

That was another cheap way to flavor the broth. Indeed, in nineteenth-century Scotland, a sheep's head was noted for making a delectable dish.[8] The basic foodstuff of ordinary people was pottage, a stew containing onions, peas and beans, and other vegetables such as leeks, garlic, roots, greens, and herbs that lay to hand. It was thickened with cereals and flavored with a bone or a piece of meat. No oven was needed for this dish; it cooked for long hours on a fire. Numerous illustrations of the time show large or small pots gently simmering thus. Irish and Scottish people today still recall with pleasure the flavor and nourishment of pottage, and it is an anachronism to regard pottage as dull and monotonous. That viewpoint reflects our changed cooking practices (long, slow cooking is a thing of the past), forgotten flavors, and our lack of direct experience of such dishes. In Shakespeare's day, pottage was even featured at the tables of the wealthy, for it was both tasty and warming. There, of course, other dishes accompanied it.[9]

BREAD

Shakespeare and his contemporaries consumed many varieties of bread. Local soils and local customs, often built up over centuries, determined what was available in a given area. It became fashionable to eat white bread made from the finest flour and called manchet. The countryman probably chose it for a treat if he went to London or visited some other large town. At their daily meals, however, the majority of people ate household bread. In the north of England it was made of oats and without yeast. Depending on how the oats were mixed and cooked, the result might be more like a pancake, wafer-thin, or a flat cake. Thin oatcakes were dried on a rack on the ceiling and stored well. In the southwest, people favored rye bread, particularly if they were doing heavy work, since it stayed longest in the stomach. Rye bread also remained moist longer than other breads. It was common in the Vale of York, perhaps because the soil was well suited to growing rye. Rye loaves were actually listed in some probate inventories taken when people died. More common than rye alone was a mixture of wheat and rye, for the two cereals were regularly sown together as a winter crop.

Barley bread was also very common, particularly in areas having lighter soils, and was enjoyed for its sweetness. Barley does not rise well, and its bread is more like a solid cake. Wheat was often used as a sponge starter, however, and the barley flour was sometimes fermented for two days to help it rise. Because it was more solid, barley bread worked well as a trencher on which other food could be laid, moistening it. If it was broken up in pottage or laid in the base of a dish with other warm and liquid foods, the moistened bread was easily digestible. A favorite crop, barley had several uses: it made beer, and it could be fed to livestock and poultry. It was a sensible choice for small farmers seeking the most versatile grain.[10]

Probably the most usual bread, eaten by a majority of the people, was one made from a mixture of grains. Gervase Markham's instructions for making bread, printed in 1615, assumed that a mixture of flours would be used: wheat and barley, wheat and rye, or rye and barley. To sustain the hard labor of workers in the field, beans were added (yielding protein), and sometimes malt as well. Henry Best, who farmed in East Yorkshire, also described various mixtures used for his workers that included peas rather than beans with rye and barley; he used maslin (wheat and rye) for his own family. In smaller households the mixture would have varied according to what the housewife had ready to hand. Variety in bread flavors was the norm, a fact supported by Juan Vives's *Dialogue*s, homely conversations in Latin intended for his pupils as tests of translation. One of the dialogues discusses the quality of the bread at the table and the ways in which it could be spoiled in the making. While variety was usually appreciated, it might not always be agreeable if a miller or baker lacked professional pride in his job or if, in years of dearth, buckwheat (usually intended for fattening poultry), turnips, or even acorns (boiled to remove the bitter taste) had to be used.[11]

VEGETABLES, HERBS, AND FRUITS

The greatest change in diet that occurred in Shakespeare's day was in the eating of vegetables, herbs, and fruits. Greenstuff and fruit had traditionally been thought fit only for the poor and for those who chose the monastic life. When these foods became fashionable, however, the art of horticulture was transformed, and new and superior varieties were introduced into England. Since many laborers were needed to grow all this produce, it did not take long for knowledge of the best growing methods, and a taste for the

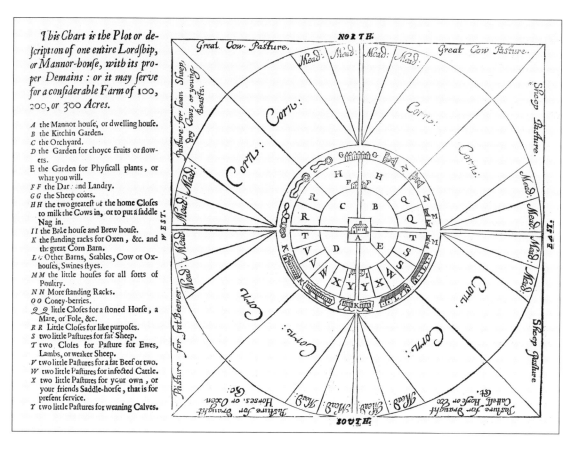

Cressy Dymock's plan for a one hundred acre farm in *A discoverie for division or setting out of land* (London, 1653), published by Samuel Hartlib.

results, to percolate through all ranks of society. This dietary revolution had geographical limits, however. It did not mean that people in every corner of England could taste and enjoy new greenstuffs and fruits. Rather, new crops spread erratically, finding a congenial countryside in parts of the kingdom and not in others. By the early seventeenth century, tithes were being paid in some areas on certain herbs, nuts, and fruits, indicating that these were now commercial items no longer grown only for domestic consumption. To understand fully the taking of such tithes, we would need to know local customs and history, but it almost certainly meant the presence nearby of a great lord or gentleman who had encountered foods in London or abroad that he wanted grown at his own home. Thus, at Great Driffield in the East Riding of Yorkshire, tithes were being demanded by 1595 on apples, pears, walnuts, filberts, warden pears, plums, damsons, onions, garlic, and red roses. Perhaps such payments to the parson may be explained by the presence of the Aumale family in a house nearby.[12]

The first signs of a changing attitude to vegetables and fruits appeared in the reign of Henry VIII. The colorful pageantry and consumerism of his court has been set vividly before our eyes by the recent publication of a full inventory of his personal goods at the time of his death. His food tastes influenced others in royal circles, and as wealth flowed more readily through an expanding economy, rich men succumbed to European fashions, welcomed the fresh interests opened up by foreign contacts, and slowly but surely changed the food at their tables. The marriage of Henry VIII to Catherine of Aragon was one significant influence, for Catherine had been brought up in Granada in southern Spain and took for granted the fine vegetables and fruits that were grown by the Moors. She was dismayed by the lack of good lettuces and cabbages in England and had to learn that such foods were despised by the rich. Henry, however, was won over to her tastes and became so greedy for globe artichokes that in 1534 he instructed the Deputy Governor, Lord de Lisle, when he visited Calais to procure all the artichokes in the vicinity for His Majesty's pleasure. In addition, in 1533 Henry ordered the planting of a royal cherry orchard at Teynham in Kent, and when Chertsey Abbey was dissolved, Henry robbed it of its finest varieties of fruit trees for Oatlands, his new palace then under construction. Henry's first daughter, Mary, was undoubtedly influenced by the tastes of her mother. Her household accounts show unusually large payments for herbs—over £8 in one bill and over £40 in another for "herbs and necessaries"—in contrast with the few pence usually paid by others.[13]

Gardeners were brought to England from France and the Netherlands in increasing numbers to grow the fruits, nuts, and vegetables that were becoming fashionable with the well-to-do. Their methods did not long remain secret. Cuttings and root stocks of improved, foreign varieties of herbs, carrots, turnips, parsnips, and green stuff passed among friends, and roots and cabbages in particular were quickly recognized as food that could sustain the poor.

Richard Gardiner, a dyer from Shrewsbury with a humanitarian concern for his hungry neighbors, fed many hundreds of people for three weeks on carrots and 700 close cabbages grown on his four acres of garden land. It was just before the new harvest, a time when bread was lacking, and was probably during the years of dearth between 1594 and 1597. He wrote a book on gardening in 1599 in which he mentioned the red carrots used in dainty salads for the rich but gave far greater emphasis to the carrots, of any kind, that could be eaten raw, broiled in butter, or stewed in pottage to fill empty stomachs. By about this same time, the end of the sixteenth century, some of the London poor had devised their own supply of

roots by growing them on the manure dumps outside the city walls, causing anxiety to city authorities about the goodness of foods grown in such places. It is worth pondering the actual flavor of carrots of the time, for Thomas Moffett called them aromatic and spicy, a description that does not fit well today.[14]

Some of the commonest vegetables—cabbages, cauliflowers, turnips, carrots, parsnips, and early peas—were being improved by the introduction of foreign varieties which arrived with Dutch and French gardeners working in England. Among the more exotic introductions were artichokes and asparagus, although when Giacomo Castelvetro offered a book of Italian cooking instructions and recipes to Lucy, Countess of Bedford, in 1614, he was not impressed with English asparagus. He had nothing but contempt for "the weedy specimens of this noble plant for sale in London." These were early days in the Englishman's learning process, however, and Castelvetro's instructions were undoubtedly of considerable practical help. He encouraged English gardeners by telling them that farmers in Verona had given up cultivating flax and wheat since their income from asparagus was three times larger.[15]

European gardeners protected their produce from the cold and frost with reed matting and made hotbeds of horse manure so it would ripen early and command the best price. These lessons were not lost on the English, and among the well-to-do there developed a strong pride in presenting foods at the table unusually early in the season, notably green peas. Foreign gardeners also taught their English neighbors to savor some herbs that the English did not use much in their dishes, although they had always used herbs freely. As John Parkinson phrased it, "The usual manner with many is to take the young buds and leaves of almost everything that groweth, as well in the garden as in the fields, and put them altogether, so that the taste of the one may amend the relish of the other." The Dutch, however, liked stronger flavors than the English, enjoyed different plants, and used them in greater quantities, sometimes stewing one herb on its own in butter in a pipkin and eating it as a separate dish. The English disparagingly called this the Dutchman's "loblolly." Yet slowly and subtly Dutch and French preferences changed the English dietary scene. If the herbs did not dramatically transform food habits, the roots and greenstuff certainly did.[16]

There was considerable uncertainty about the food value of fruits, and there was deep disagreement on the subject among a number of authors. Thomas Elyot thought that fruit caused putrid fevers if eaten too much; he felt that if apples, pears, or quinces were eaten at all they should be baked or roasted. Elyot and others who wrote in this vein often seemed to be thinking only of wild fruits, as was Thomas Tusser when he referred to crab apples, a fruit that was probably quite sour but which could be sweetened with honey or sugar during cooking. Gradually during the sixteenth century, those who traveled widely encountered improved varieties of familiar fruits and became acquainted with entirely new ones like apricots. These are said to have been introduced to England in 1529 by one of Henry VIII's gardeners, the Frenchman John Woolf. Slowly cultured Englishmen began to soften their prejudices against fruit in general. William Harrison plainly enjoyed the experience of what he called "delicate" apples and other fruit, and Thomas Moffett expressed regret that poor people had to rely on wild crabs and pears from the hedgerows when warden pears (an improved, cultivated kind) were so much more nourishing. Moffett viewed fruit more positively than some others because he knew that many people in Asia, Africa, and India relied on fruit and lived long lives.[17] A further testimony to England's pleasure in eating fruit is found in James I's answer to his doctor, Theodore Mayerne, in 1618 when James was asked about his food. He replied that he ate fruit at all hours of the day and night and recalled, in particular, one large meal of cherries.[18]

As more attention was given to fruit, certain counties of England, such as Herefordshire, Worcestershire, Devon, and Kent, were noticed because of the unusual quantities of fruit growing there, much of it in hedgerows. This distinctive feature of some local landscapes (not set there deliberately enough to be called a specialty) must have crept in stealthily over the centuries because congenial soil conditions and climate permitted the trees to spread and because country people left free-growing plants and trees alone if they did not need the land for other purposes. Once people tasted foreign fruits, however, they began to compare the good fruits from abroad with their much inferior specimens. Gervase Markham cheerfully acknowledged the superiority of French fruit: "We are as farre from their fruits as they are from our wools," he declared.[19] Horatio Busino, an Italian visitor in England, put it more strongly, judging English pears as "scarcely eatable" and "the other fruits most abominable, their taste resembling that of insipid masticated grass." In Italy Busino could enjoy numerous different kinds of cherries, whereas the English had only one kind, bad morello cherries, he claimed. More significant still was his remark that fruit was not a food eaten sedately at mealtimes in England; the English ate their fruit in the streets, like goats. In other words, fruit had not yet found a sure place at the meal table.[20]

So, a more discerning appreciation of fruit developed gradually in England, assisted by nobility and gentry, their foreign gardeners, and foreign plants. Who knows what influences of the time caused the clerk of Barnstaple in North Devon, when he was ostensibly recording notable events in the town in 1590, to write about an agreeably abundant harvest of cherries gathered that year, including masers (the dark red variety)? And how long, we may wonder, had Berkshire people around Harwell enjoyed an annual crop of cherries when, in 1617, one of their gentlemen farmers, Robert Loder, noted in his farm account the picking of nearly 5,000 pounds in his orchards? He even worked out the exact proportion eaten in his household, the amount eaten by his pickers, and the amount sold.[21]

Fruit eating was becoming a qualitatively different experience than in the past, and the gentry passed through phases of enthusiasm for various modish foods. A more careful scrutiny of surviving documents and illustrations might well produce a significant list in some sort of chronological order. Walnuts would surely be at the height of fashion for two generations from about 1600 onwards. The planting of great numbers of walnut trees plainly occurred in the Elizabethan and early Stuart period. Was it due more to a liking for the appearance of the trees in parkland, or to the wood for furniture, or was it simply because of the nuts? Certainly great numbers of nuts were pickled while others matured into dessert fruit. By the early eighteenth century, Croydon in Surrey was celebrating an annual walnut fair in the autumn which drew thousands of people from London.[22]

The success that gentlemen had in growing apricots and peaches prompts further reflections on fashion and its priorities in different decades of the seventeenth century. A chronology of the court's preferences would show that around 1600 infinite care was taken to protect exotic fruit trees in winter using glass screens, coverts, and heated walls. In fact, the fruit-growing ambitions of the wealthy knew no bounds at the time. When Sir Francis Carew awaited a visit from Queen Elizabeth to his house at Beddington in Surrey, he managed to delay the ripening of his cherries by spreading a tent over the trees for two to three weeks and watering it regularly. The tent was removed at just the right moment for the cherries to ripen as the queen arrived. When James I and his queen celebrated the making of peace between England and Spain at a banquet in Whitehall in 1604, James handed to his principal guest, the Constable of Castile, a melon and six oranges still hanging on a green branch. These were the fruit of Spain, he said,

now transplanted into England. It is likely that the oranges came from Sir Francis Carew's garden, for he is known to have grown orange trees outdoors under a covert. Indeed, he is said to have been the first to grow them at all. But it was a matter of pride rather than need; considerable quantities of oranges were imported into England from Spain in the sixteenth and early seventeenth centuries. Forty thousand oranges arrived in London in one cargo in January, 1568, and oranges were being eaten as far away as Naworth Castle, Cumberland, by Lord William Howard in 1620.[23]

Country people's familiarity with wild or with more exotic varieties of fruit varied from place to place, as did their knowledge of vegetables and herbs. A new interest had been awakened, however, and gardeners were permitted by the terms of their contracts with their gentlemen employers to dispose of their surplus where they liked. Sir Arthur Throckmorton, Walter Raleigh's brother-in-law, made such a contract with his gardener in 1611, so it is fair to guess that fruits as well as vegetables passed among neighbors along with roots and cuttings.[24]

DAIRY PRODUCTS

The place of dairy products in people's diet did not undergo any significant change in Shakespeare's day. It was not until the second half of the seventeenth century that commercial production surged noticeably in certain dairying districts. Liquid milk, buttermilk and whey, butter, and cheese had always been regarded as the mainstay of poor people while they were said to form only a small part of the diet of the rich.[25] It is difficult, however, to arrive at an all-embracing general view. Dairy produce might not seem conspicuous at the tables of the gentry, but it was much used in the kitchen. Probate inventories suggest that domestic consumption among ordinary folk was high. Among those having land, no matter what their class, a cow was deemed the first necessity. Milk was strongly commended to the young, the old, and the sick

Women preserving fruit, from Nicholas de Bonnefons, *The French gardiner, instructing how to cultivate all sorts of fruit-trees* (London, 1658).

in all classes of society, although men were thought to need something more as well. On a visit to England in 1599, Thomas Platter discovered that milk was a routine drink. Pausing for refreshment between Canterbury and Sitting-bourne in Kent, he was startled to be given not ale or beer but a tankard of milk.[26]

Thomas Moffett described butter as the chief food of the poor, an odd remark unless he meant that the poor did not have the same access as he did to the fat and drippings of meat. Even so, he seems to have been oddly oblivious to the use of butter in cooking in manorial kitchens. Perhaps his point of view is understandable, however, when we appreciate how often manorial gentry relied on deliveries of butter and cheese to their back doors by local small farmers. If they had no dairy in their own manor houses, dairying might be an activity of which the gentry saw little. This also meant that the quality of the produce was variable and could be distinctly poor or very good. Some villagers did become locally renowned for supplying delectable varieties of both cheese and butter.[27]

Cheese as a food was regarded with ambivalence. Thomas Cogan thought it good for laborers but not for students. Thomas Venner (1620) thought it engendered ill humors but could see that it was convenient for "rustic people" with strong stomachs who took plenty of exercise. More delicate digestions, including those of scholars, were not wholly denied the eating of cheese, but it was to be eaten in moderation and always after other meat. Thus, at the end of one meal in *The Merry Wives of Windsor* (1.2.12), the pippins and cheese were announced as yet to come.[28]

At the same time, however, cheese was moving up the social scale. Some gentlewomen closely supervised their own domestic dairies, and it is not impossible that foreign influences broadened and deepened their practical interest. One elaborate meal eaten in a monastery in Madrid in 1626, and described in detail by the cupbearer of the papal legate, Francesco Barberini, included so many slices of cheese that they covered the whole plate. If English people abroad witnessed similar scenes, they may well have developed a higher appreciation of cheeses. Londoners also had the opportunity to savor foreign cheeses at home since they were imported regularly from Holland. Parmesan, Angelot, and Auvergne cheeses are mentioned in surviving documents, even those reporting quite casual conversations. Moffett gives us a precious glimpse of his niece copying the Angelot cheeses of Normandy and producing something that in his judgement surpassed them.[29]

BEVERAGES

As with food, so too with drink. Innumerable alternatives were available to all classes, and every household must have had its own favorite flavors and mixtures. Many involved no expenditure of money but called only for the housewife's effort, interest, and skill in combining herbs or spices to add agreeable flavors to water, ale, and beer. Ale and beer were not always made from barley. Oats, rye (in Cornwall), and sometimes mixtures including wheat were also used. Ale and beer were undoubtedly the preferred choice of the menfolk, and they were joyfully anticipated by all at festive occasions. They were also safer for everyone when water supplies were impure, so modest housewives regularly brewed at home. One laborer, testifying in a legal dispute, declared roundly that while he usually drank ale or beer, he, his wife, and five children drank water when he had no money. He failed to mention any herbal flavorings his wife probably added to the water, taking such subtle culinary extras for granted. Syrups were made of virtually every herb and flower and were watered down as drinks while barley water was made from the commonest cereal in the kitchen.

In the fruit growing areas of the West Midlands and southwest (Herefordshire, Gloucestershire, Somerset, and Devon), and in Kent too, cider was a common drink, but until the 1640s, when the royalists encountered it and it began to be fashionable, it was dismissed as the poor drink of country folk, not for connoisseurs. Fermenting and distillation were common practices in the houses of the gentry, and made drinks' refreshing and medicinal properties were so entangled in people's minds that they could not be separated. "Diet drinks" containing herbs with a restorative medicinal reputation appeared regularly in household accounts, and not necessarily in a fermented liquor.

Farming folk drank plenty of full cream milk from their own domestic cows, freely giving the whey and buttermilk from the dairy to their poorer neighbors since these liquids were regarded as valueless waste. In harsh winter weather, possets (spiced drinks of milk, curdled with ale or wine and sometimes thickened almost to a pottage consistency), cawdles (of ale with egg yolks, sugar, or honey), and spicy drinks were most welcome if served hot, but it may be that people generally drank many more cold liquids than hot ones. Consequently, when coffee, chocolate, and tea arrived on the scene in the second half of the seventeenth century, they were seen as novelties for more than one reason.[30] We get a glimpse of the prejudices they induced in a sour comment by William Cobbett in the nineteenth century, when agricultural laborers had also developed the taste for tea. They were always arriving late for work, he said, claiming that they had had to wait for the kettle to boil; breakfast beer in Shakespeare's day was ready in a moment.[31]

It was not until the 1650s that the first coffee and chocolate drinks were introduced by English travelers who had been to Turkey and the West Indies. Coffee found its first home in a coffee house in Oxford in 1650 and in one in London in 1652; chocolate was introduced to London in 1657. Drinking these beverages went hand-in-hand with animated conversation in public houses where one could also pick up news of the latest projects in town. Some nobility and gentry were freely drinking coffee at home by the 1670s and 1680s while chocolate as a drink lost ground to cocoa but was soon in demand as a confectionery. One London coffee house was selling tea from China by 1658, although the best method for preparing tea long remained uncertain. Sir Kenelm Digby passed on a recipe from a Jesuit in China about 1660 which added egg yolks and sugar to the infused tea.[32]

These were turbulent times in the shaping of a confident philosophy about food and health. Contemporary theorists were far from agreeing on the goodness of many foods, and this is to be expected since both domestic households and the market supplied such a variety regionally and socially. Wider public knowledge of foods that had long been eaten in areas throughout the kingdom, plus a deepening acquaintance with foods newly arriving on the scene, meant that there was a bewildering array of foods to experience. In addition, Shakespeare and his contemporaries lived in a world in which the rich were plainly getting richer while the poorest, without roofs over their heads and begging for food from door to door, were disturbingly conspicuous in both town and country. Criticisms of overeating, greed, and gluttony therefore come as no surprise, although Shakespeare seems not to have been unduly preoccupied with such matters. The words "glutton," "gluttony," and "gluttonous" occcur only six times in all the plays, and when they do occur they are often used in a metaphorical sense. But, thoughtful men brooded uneasily on the modish desire for variety in food and recommended moderation in its consumption. Those who observed the world around them suggested that simple food and drink might be more conducive to health and long life than a rich surfeit. Fifty years later the debate seems to have died away, and Robert May's recipe book (1660) demonstrates that variety was being achieved in simpler ways as people varied their basic recipes and modestly added diverse flavorings.[33]

NOTES

1 Werner Rösener, *The Peasantry of Europe* (Oxford, 1994), 149.

2 Thomas Moffett, *Health's Improvement* (London, 1655), passim, but especially 101–102, 110–117, 141ff. Moffett wrote this book c1595.

3 Moffett, passim, but especially 92, 98, 101; L. Mascall, *The Countreyman's Jewell: or The Government of Cattel*, enlarged edition (London, 1680), 386. Mascall died in 1589.

4 Todd Gray, ed., *Devon Household Accounts, 1627–59*, Part 1, Devon and Cornwall Record Society, NS 38, 1–110, especially 20–21, 36, 99.

5 Moffett, 77.

6 British Library, Sloane MS, 2117, fol. 208.

7 Elizabeth Grey, Countess of Kent, *A True Gentlewoman's Delight, wherein is contained all Manner of Cookery* (London, 1653), 18; British Library, Sloane MS, 2117, fol. 81v.

8 Joan Thirsk, ed., *The Agrarian History of England and Wales*, IV: 1500–1640 (Cambridge, 1967), xxxv; William Harrison, *The Description of England*, ed. George Edelen (Washington and New York, 1994), 127; W. B. Rye, *England as Seen by Foreigners* (London, 1865), 152; Ida Macalpine and Richard Hunter, *George III and the Mad Business* (New York, 1969), 203; Lorna Weatherill, ed., *The Account Book of Richard Latham, 1724–67*, British Academy, *Records of Social and Economic History*, NS 15 (1990), 139, 145, 147, 153, 162; Olive M. Geddes, *The Laird's Kitchen. Three Hundred Years of Food in Scotland* (Edinburgh, 1994), 47, 92, 93.

9 Pottage appears in the cookbook of Robert May, *The Accomplisht Cook, or The Art and Mystery of Cookery* (facsimile of 1685 edition), ed. Alan Davidson (Totnes, 1994), 93–95, 422.

10 Tobias Venner, *Via Recta ad Vitam Longam, or A Plaine Philosophical Discourse of the Nature, Faculties, and Effects…for the Preservation of Health* (London, 1620), 17–21; Moffett, 235ff; F. Atkinson, "Oatbread of Northern England," *Gwerin*, III (1960–1962), 44ff; Marie Hartley and Joan Ingilby, *Making Oatcake* (Otley, 1998), passim; Hilary Spurling, *Elinor Fettiplace's Receipt Book. Elizabethan Country House Cooking* (Harmondsworth, 1987), 92–93.

11 Gervase Markham, *The English Housewife*, ed. Michael R. Best (Montreal and Kingston, 1994), 209–211; Harrison, 135; Donald Woodward, ed., *The Farming and Memorandum Books of Henry Best of Elmswell, 1642*, British Academy, *Records of Social and Economic History*, NS VIII (1984), 109; Juan Vives, *Tudor Schoolboy Life*, ed. Foster Watson (London, 1970), 133–135 (A more informative translation as regards bread is found in the Spanish version: Juan Vives, *Diálogos*, 4th ed. (Madrid, 1959), 88–89. The work was originally published in 1538.); Hugh Platt, *Sundrie New and Artificiall Remedies against Famine* (London, 1596), A4v–B2r.

12 Joan Thirsk, *Alternative Agriculture. A History from the Black Death to the Present Day* (Oxford, 1997), 35–36, 272, note 40.

13 Harrison, 264; David Starkey, ed., *The Inventory of Henry VIII* (London, 1998); H. M. Colvin, *The History of the King's Works, IV: 1485–1660, Part II* (London, 1982), 213; Thirsk, *Alternative Agriculture*, 31–32; *Letters and Papers of Henry VIII, Vol. IV, Part 1, 1524–26*, 710.

14 Malcolm Thick, *The Neat House Gardens. Early Market Gardening around London* (Totnes, 1998), 19–23; Idem, "Root crops and the feeding of London's poor in the late sixteenth and early seventeenth centuries," in J. Chartres and David Hey, eds., *English Rural Society, 1500–1800* (Cambridge, 1990), passim, but especially 287, 290–292; British Library, Lansdowne MS 74, fol. 75–76; Moffett, 218.

15 Thick, *Neat House Gardens*, 23, 61–64; Gillian Riley, ed., *The Fruit, Herbs, and Vegetables of Italy* (London, 1989), 53–54.

16 John Parkinson, *Paradisi in Sole, Paradisus Terrestris* (London, 1629), 468–469, 494, 496, 500, 510.

17   Sir Thomas Elyot, *The Castel of Helth* (London, 1541), 23v; Thomas Tusser, *Five Hundred Points of Good Husbandry*, ed. G. Grigson (Oxford, 1984), 27; John Dent, *The Quest for Nonsuch* (London, 1912), 114; Harrison, 269; Moffett, 194–195, 214.

18   Macalpine and Hunter, 203, 207.

19   Cited by Lynette Hunter in "'Sweet Secrets' from occasional receipt to specialised books: the growth of a genre," in C. Anne Wilson, ed., *Banquetting Stuffe* (Edinburgh, 1991), 53.

20   *Calendar of State Papers Venetian, 1617-19*, 319.

21   Todd Gray, *The Lost Chronicle of Barnstaple, 1586–1611* (Barnstaple, 1998), 67; G. E. Fussell, ed., *Robert Loder's Farm Accounts, 1610–1620*, Camden Society, Third Series, LIII (1936), 133.

22   Thirsk, *Alternative Agriculture*, 57. Moffett, 195, noted the large apricots that were grown against the kitchen chimney wall at Barn Elms, along the Thames. This was almost certainly a reference to the house of Sir Francis Walsingham.

23   Hugh Platt, *The Jewell House of Art and Nature* (London, 1594), 5; Idem, *The Garden of Eden* (London, 1653), 165. The orange trees at Beddington were said in 1722 to have been growing there for more than a hundred years, planted in open ground under a movable covert that was brought into use during the winter months. W. Camden, *Britannia*, 2d ed., ed. Edmund Gibson, I (London, 1722), 191; W. B. Rye, 118–120; B. Dietz, ed., *The Port and Trade of Early Elizabethan London. Documents*, London Record Society (1972), no. 277; Rev. George Ornsby, ed., *Selections from the Household Books of the Lord William Howard of Naworth Castle*, Surtees Society, 68 (1877), 136.

24   A. L. Rowse, *Ralegh and the Throckmortons* (London, 1964), 283.

25   Thirsk, *Alternative Agriculture*, 48–49; Harrison, 126.

26   Moffett, 119, 125; Thirsk, *Agrarian History*, IV, xxxv.

27   Moffett, 129; Sir Thomas Elyot, 34r, 23r; Ornsby, 84.

28   Thomas Cogan, *The Haven of Health* (London, 1584), 159; Venner, 91–92.

29   María del Carmen Simón Palmer, *La Alimentación y sus Circunstancias en el Real Alcázar de Madrid*, Instituto de Estudios Madrileños (Madrid, 1982), 23–24; Joan Thirsk, *Economic Policy and Projects. The Development of a Consumer Society in Early Modern England* (Oxford, 1978), 182; St. Clare Byrne, *The Elizabethan Home* (London, 1949), 33, 70; Dietz, no. 110; Moffett, 133.

30   Imported wines are a large subject not dealt with here, although a contemporary list is given in Raphael Holinshed, *England in the Sixteenth Century* (London, 1913), 63–64. For home-produced drinks, see C. Anne Wilson, *Food and Drink in Britain* (London, 1991), 372–413; Spurling, 63–64, 78, 214–217. For contemporary comments, see Harrison, 135–140. For a wealth of seventeenth-century recipes (not published until 1669), see *The Closet of Sir Kenelm Digby Knight Opened*, ed. Anne Macdonell (London, 1910), 5–110.

31   William Cobbett, *Cottage Economy* (London, 1926), 21.

32   Wilson, *Food and Drink in Britain*, 405–413.

33   Moffett, 232, 258, 260–284; Burton Stevenson, *Stevenson's Book of Shakespeare Quotations* (London, 1938), 236; Elyot, 32v, 34r, 41–42.

October hath 31 dayes

Yee flowers all of brauest blee ✻ Must vnto winter now giue place ✻
O happy heart, from out of which ✻ The feare of God all sinne doth chase

December hath 31 dayes

The Sunne now in the lowest course ✻ Makes longest night, and shortest day ✻
In fine God bring vs to the place ✻ wher bright day light shall shine alway

Day	breaketh.	Sunne	ryseth	Sunne	setteth.	Twylight	
houre	minut.	houre	minut	houre	minut	houre	minut.
5	58	8	12	3	48	6	2

The day is 7 houres long and 36 minuts The night is 16 houres long and 24 minut

Now colde December is come in ✻ And poore mans back is clothed thin ✻
Feede and cloth him then as ye may ✻ The Lord wyll it three-folde repay ✻

CATALOGUE OF THE EXHIBITION

Mary Anne Caton
with Ronald W. Fuchs, II

Left: Providing hospitality to a guest, the illustration
for December from Thomas Trevelyon's Pictorial
commonplace book (Manuscript, 1608).

CHAP. I.

1. *What Diet is.*
2. *Who were the authors of it.*
3. *What good it bringeth.*

Iet is defined by very learned Scholars, an exact order in Labour, Meat, Drink, Sleep, and Venery. For they are thought to be *Pythagoras* his pentangle or five-squar'd figure, wherein (as *Hipocrates* saith of mans body) there be several confluences and concurrences; yet but one general Sympathy through all Neverthelefs Labor was appointed for moft to invite meat and drink: they to draw on fleep, for the eafe of our labours: and all four, to perfit generation; which is not onely *effendi sed semper essendi causa*; *not onely the caufe of being but of ever being*: for indeed after we are dead in our felves, we recover in our pofterity another life. But in this Treatife I define Diet more particularly (as it is ufually taken both by the vulgar and also the beft Phyfitians) to be an orderly and due courfe obferved in the ufe of bodily nourifhments, for the prefervation recovery or continuance of the health of mankind. Which how and when it was firft invented and by whom

Biefius lib. i. theor med.
Iafon Prait lib. 1. Diet.
Hippr c.lib d◦. Princ.

Ariftot. lib de gen. anim.

Gal.cap. 2. lib. 11. Comm.
Hippoc. de that.hum.
Avicen. lib.1. Top.3.cap.7.
All our life is but a confumption.

B
col-

Thomas Moffett (1553–1604)

Healths improvement; or rules comprizing and discovering the nature, method, and manner of preparing all sorts of food used in this nation

London, 1655

Shelf mark: M2382

(illustrated at left)

Diet, according to Moffett, is an orderly course of nourishment "for the preservation recovery or continuance of the health of mankind." In thirty-two chapters, Moffett divides all foods into five groups: meats of beasts and birds; dairy products (including curds, whey, eggs, and blood); sea- and fresh-water fish; fruits of orchard, garden, and field; and various breads. Flavorings (salt, sugar, and spice), sauces, and finally, the time, order, and manner of eating conclude the book. The correct preparation of meals and medicines took into account not only the patient's own humor, but also that of her food. Harvesting greens and herbs depended on the positions of the sun, moon, and stars, as herbal humors varied depending on what hour of the day the herbs were picked. Arguing that a good diet prolongs life, Moffett counsels specific diets for the young, the healthy, and the seriously ill.

Thomas Tryon (1634–1703)

A treatise of cleanness in meats and drinks: of the preparation of food, and the excellency of good airs, and the benefits of clean sweet beds. Also of the generation of bugs, and their cure, to which is added, a short discourse of the pain in the teeth, shewing from what cause it does chiefly proceed, and also how to prevent it

London, 1682

Shelf mark: T3196

With his "discourse of the pain in the teeth," Thomas Tryon hopes to educate his readers about the importance of "continual cleansing and washing." Tracing gum disease and tooth decay to "the continual eating of Flesh, and of fat, sweet things. . .which do not only obstruct the stomach, but fur and foul the mouth," Tryon argues that speedy digestion prevents corruption of teeth and gums. Eight points about dental care complement earlier chapters on food preparation. He especially recommends

> *every Morning to wash your Mouth with at least ten or twelve Mouthfuls of pure Water, cold from the Spring or River, and so again after Dinner and Supper, swallowing down a Mouthful of Water after each Washing: For there is no sort of Liquor in the World so pure and clean as Water. . . .*

Tryon praises shepherds and husbandmen for their knowledge of nature. His belief in a moderate, vegetable-based diet and in abstinence from alcohol reflects his Anabaptist sobriety and appears throughout his sixteen books on health.

Jean Prevost (1585–1631)

Medicaments for the Poor; or, physick for the common people, containing excellent remedies for most common diseases incident to man's body; made of such things as are common to be had in almost every country in the world; and are made with a little art, and final charge.

Translated into English by Nicholas Culpeper

London, 1656

Shelf mark: P3324.8

Prevost itemizes the types and degrees of evacuation, each according to the part of the body treated. As all foods, cooked or raw, corresponded to one of the four humors (blood, choler, phlegm, or melancholy), so did medicines administered to balance the body's

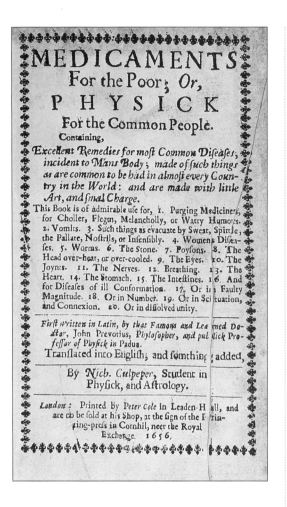

Containing,

Excellent Remedies for moſt Common Diſeaſes, incident to Mans Body; made of ſuch things as are common to be had in almoſt every Coun-try in the World: and are made with little Art, and ſmal Charge.

This Book is of admirable uſe for, 1. Purging Medicines, for Choller, Flegm, Melancholly, or Watry Humors. 2. Vomits. 3. Such things as evacuate by Sweat, Spittle, the Pallate, Noſtrils, or Inſenſibly. 4. Womens Diſea-ſes. 5. Worms. 6. The Stone. 7. Poyſons. 8. The Head over-heat, or over-cooled. 9. The Eyes. 10. The Joynts. 11. The Nerves. 12. Breathing. 13. The Heart. 14. The Stomach. 15. The Inteſtines. 16. And for Diſeaſes of ill Conformation. 17. Or in a Faulty Magnitude. 18. Or in Number. 19. Or in Scituation, and Connexion. 20. Or in diſſolved unity.

Firſt written in Latin, by that Famous and Learned Do-ctor, John Prevotius, Phyloſopher, and publick Pro-feſſor of Phyſick in Padua.

Tranſlated into Engliſh, and ſomthing added,

By Nich. Culpeper, Student in Phyſick, and Aſtrology.

London: Printed By Peter Cole in Leaden-Hall, and are to be ſold at his Shop, at the ſign of the Prin-ting-preſs in Cornhil, neer the Royal Exchange. 1656.

Culpeper's aim is "not to give over, until I have published in English whatsoever shal be necessary to make an Industrious, Diligent, Rational Man a knowing Physician." He discusses how medicines can be made easily from natural ingredients to save money, or for speedy relief while traveling.

A book of fruits and flowers. Shewing the nature and use of them, for meat or medicine
London, 1653
Shelf mark: 230165
(illustrated at right)

In most recipe books, a broad variety of recipes for main courses (pies, sallets, "fritterstuffe"), banqueting dishes (marchpanes, "sugar-workes," snow) and medi-cines (distilled waters to treat wounds, salves to treat aches) appeared side by side. Also included might be recipes for medicines compounded from fruits and flowers for the treatment of more serious diseases like consumptions, ruptures, ulcers, and kidney stones. Each plant's properties as an oil, a syrup, a conserve, a paste, or a powder would be elaborated. Violet oil, for example, helped to ease a melancholy humor. The recipe for violet syrup included in this book calls for nineteen ounces of stamped violets boiled in one pound of sugar; when cooled and dissolved in almond milk, it treated inflammation in children.

humors. Purges, medicaments, clysters, cordials, and other remedies for diseases combined herbs, flowers, or garden plants with oil, sugar, and flower juices.

Like sugar, vegetables were perceived as an unusual specialty and first became known to many people as medicines. Coleworts (plants in the cabbage family) were a crop imported from The Netherlands and were initially considered good food for the poor because of their food value. Among the greens thought to "loosen the belly in a flegmatick case," colewort was given as juice, broth, or boiled with oil and salt. Other remedies included oat meal in gruel, chick pea or lentil broth, the broth of all salt fish, dry figs soaked in milk or wine, bran bread, new walnuts, and "the decoction of sweet cods (peas)." Such medicines were often given as breakfast (see Hannah Woolley) or as the first food of the day. Others, like broiled capers, were eaten in "sallets" with vinegar or as a sauce for another dish.

Mary Granville (fl. c1646–1669)

or Ann Granville Dewes (fl. c1740)
Cookery and medicinal recipes
Manuscript, England and Spain, c1640–1750
Shelf mark: V.a. 430

Like many housewives, Ann received her cookery book from her mother, Mary Granville, possibly as a marriage gift. The Granvilles lived in Cadiz and Malaga, Spain, in the mid-seventeenth century, so many of their recipes are associated with a particular source or place. The mixture of medicines and cookery reflects the wife's role as the family's care-giver and her responsibility for the preparation of distilled waters, ointments, and other medicines. Dr. Burges's cure for

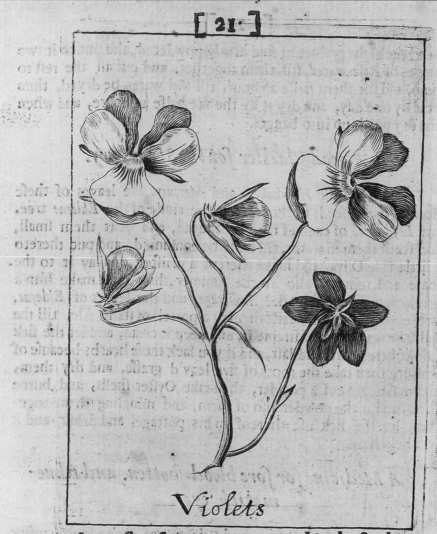

Violets

To make Paſte of Violets, or any kind of Flowers.

Take your Flowers, pick them, and ſtamp them in an *Alablaſter* morter, then ſteep them two howres in a ſauſer of *Roſe*-water, after ſtraine it, and ſteep a little *Gum Dragon* in the ſame water, then beat it to paſt, print it in your Moulds, and it will be of the very colour and taſt of the Flowers, then gild them, and ſo you may have every Flower in his owne colour, and taſt better for the mouth, then any printed colour.

Powder of Violets.

Take ſweet *Ireos* roots one ounce, red *Roſes* two ounces, *Storax* one ounce and a halfe, *Cloves* two drams, *Marjerome* one dram, *Lavinder* flowers one dram and a halfe, make theſe into powder;
           then

the plague and Dr. Chambers's water contrast with medicines for sore breasts and nipples. One example of the latter uses new milk, a penny loaf, saffron, and grease. (Dewes, 3) Leonard Wilkes's recipe for good chocolate is one of the few recipes for drink. Commenting on her recipe for pigeon or lark fricassee, Granville writes, "I thinke that lemon will be better than vinegar [to beat the meat and egg yolks in]." (Dewes, 25)

Ointment Pot
Tin-glazed earthenware
England, 1675–1700
Courtesy of Plimoth Plantation,
70.462
(illustrated below)

Tin-glazed earthenware ointment pots such as this one, also known as galley pots after the rowed galleys that first brought them to England, were intended for ointments, salves, and other medicines or cosmetics. Their design and decoration seem to have originated in the Middle East in the twelfth century and to have

Courtesy of Plimoth Plantation.
Photograph by Ted Curtin.

reached England via Italy and the Low Countries by 1567, when John Stow reports that

> *Jasper Andries and Jacob Janson, potters, came away from Antwerp to avoid the persecution there, and settled themselves in Norwich, where they followed their trade, making gally paving tiles, and vessels for apothecaries very artificially."* (Stow, 327)

Archaeological excavations in England and America show that ointment pots were made in vast quantities. Such pots could be bought filled at an apothecary's shop and were probably recycled for homemade concoctions such as Markham's recipe for "an ointment for burning" that called for the ingredients to be boiled, stirred, and strained "into clean pots." (Markham, 37) The earliest ointment pots were painted in polychrome colors, while those made in the mid- to late-seventeenth century were decorated in purple and blue.

William Bullein (d. 1576)
Bulleins bulwarke of defence against all sicknesse, sorenesse, and woundes that doe dayly assualte mankinde… Gathered and practised from the most worthy learned, both olde and new: to the great comfort of mankind: by William Bullein, Doctor of Physick
London, 1579
Shelf mark: STC 4034
(illustrated at right)

William Bullein considered himself "a chylde of the Common Wealth" whose duty was to help the ignorant. (Bullein, Cii) He called Thomas Elyot's *The Castel of Helthe* a worthy example to follow and wrote his own guide, first published in 1562, while he was imprisoned for debt. One of the treatise's four parts, the "Booke of simples," is among the earliest English herbals. Garden plants in Bullein's index of simples include strawberry, cherry, radish, and walnut. Chickenweed, one of the plants illustrated here, is, according to John Gerard's *Herball*, cold and moist and good to treat ulcers and ease swollen legs. (Gerard, 615)

An Index of the booke of Simples.

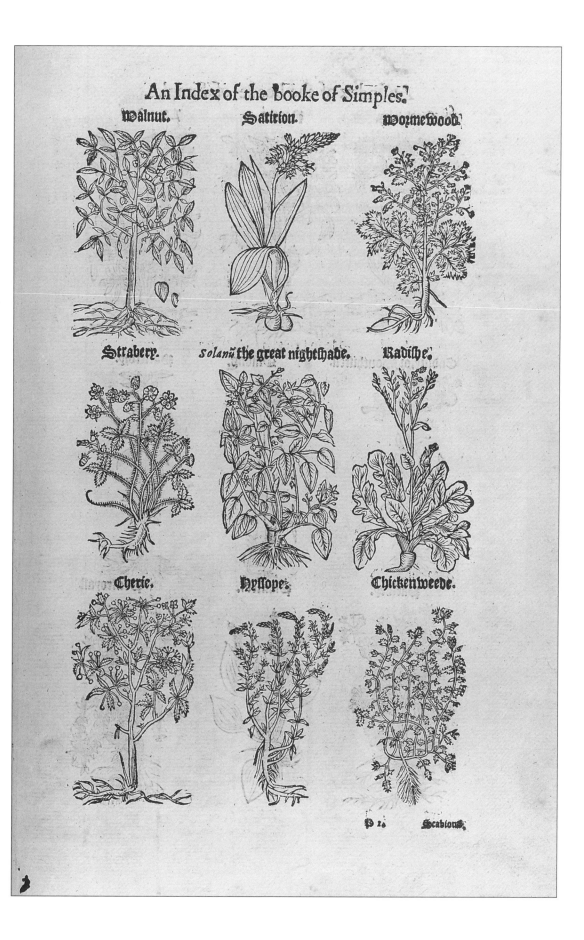

walnut.   Satirion.   wormewood.

Strabery.   solanū the great nightshade.   Radishe.

Cherie.   Hyssope.   Chickenweede.

P 2.   Scabious.

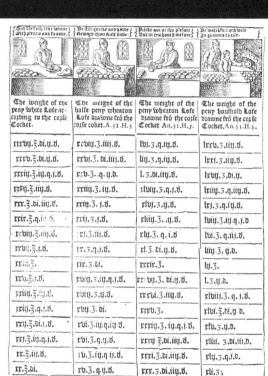

The price of the quarter of wheate.	The weight of the half peny white Loafe drawn from the fine Cocket. An.51.H.3	The weight of the peny white Loafe drawne frō the fine Cocket. An.51.H.3.	The weight of the half peny white Lofe drawne frō the corse Cocket. An.51.H.3.	The weight of the peny white Lofe according to the corse Cocket.	The weight of the halfe peny wheaton Lofe drawne frō the corse coket. A.51.H.3	The weight of the peny wheaton Lofe drawne frō the corse Cocket. An.51.H.3.	The weight of the peny houshold Lofe drawne frō the corse Cocket. An.51.H.3.
ix s.	xviij. ℥. iij. q. iij. ꝺ.	xxxvi. ℥. iij. q. j. ꝺ.	xviij. ℥. iij. q. j. ꝺ.	xxxvij. ℥. ꝺi. j. ꝺ.	xlvij. ℥. iiij. ꝺ.	lvj. ℥. q. iij. ꝺ.	lxxb. ℥. iij. ꝺ.
ix.s.vi.ꝺ.	xbij. ℥. q. iij. ꝺ.	xxxiiij. ℥ iij.q.iij. ꝺ.	xbij. ℥. iij. q. j. ꝺ.	xxxj. ℥. ꝺi. iiij. ꝺ.	liij. ℥. q. iij. ꝺ.	lxxj. ℥. iij. ꝺ.
x s.	xbj. ℥. ꝺi. ij. ꝺ.	xxxiij. ℥ iiij. ꝺ.	xbj. ℥. iij. q. iij. ꝺ.	xxriij. ℥. ij. q. ij. ꝺ.	l. ℥. ꝺi. iiij. ꝺ.	lxbij. ℥. ꝺi. ij.
x.℥.vi.ꝺ.	xb. ℥. iij. q.	xxxi. ℥. ꝺi.	xbj. ℥. ij. ꝺ.	xxbj. ℥. iiij. ꝺ.	xlbiij. ℥. q. j. ꝺ.	lxiiij. ℥. q. iiij. ꝺ.
xi.s.	xb. ℥. j. ꝺ.	xxx. ℥. ij. ꝺ.	xb. ℥. q. ij. ꝺ.	xxir. ℥. ꝺi. iiij. ꝺ.	xlbj. ℥. ij. ꝺ.	lxj. ℥. q. iij. ꝺ.
xi.℥.bi.ꝺ.	xiiij. ℥. q. iiij. ꝺ.	xxbiij. ℥ iij. q. j. ꝺ.	xiiij. ℥. ꝺi. iiij. ꝺ.	xxir. ℥. q. iij. ꝺ.	xxbj. ℥. j. ꝺ.	xliij. ℥. ij. q. ꝺ.	lbiij. ℥. iij. q. j. ꝺ.
xij.s.	xiij. ℥. iiij. ꝺ.	xxbj. ℥. ꝺi. iij. ꝺ.	xiiij. ℥. ij. ꝺ.	xrbiij. ℥. iij. q. ꝺ.	xt.j. ℥. iij. ꝺ.	xlij. ℥. q. j. ꝺ.	lbi. ℥. q. iij. ꝺ.
xij.℥.vi.ꝺ.	xij. ℥. ꝺi. iiij. ꝺ.	xxbj. ℥. q. iij. ꝺ.	xiiij. ℥. j. ꝺ.	xrbj. ℥. j. q. ꝺ.	xr. ℥. j. ꝺ.	rl. ℥. ꝺi. ij. ꝺ.	liiij. ℥. ij. ꝺ.
xiij.℥.	xij. ℥. q.	xxiiij. ℥. ꝺi.	xij. ℥. ꝺi. ob.	xxr. ℥. ꝺi.	rir. ℥. ꝺi.	rrr. ℥. ꝺi. iiij. ꝺ.	lij. ℥.
xiiij.s.	xj. ℥. iij. q. j. ꝺ.	xxiiij. ℥. ꝺi. ij. ꝺ.	xij. ℥. j. ꝺ. ob.	xrb. ℥. ꝺi. iij. ꝺ.	xbiij. ℥. ij. q. j. ꝺ.	rr biij. ℥. ꝺi. ij. ꝺ.	l. ℥. iij. ꝺ.
xiiij.℥.bi.ꝺ.	xj. ℥. q. ij. ꝺ.	xiij. ℥. iij. q. j. ꝺ.	xj. ℥. iij. ꝺ. iij. ꝺ.	xriij. ℥. j. q. ꝺ.	xbiij. ℥. q. ꝺ.	rrbj. ℥. iiij. ꝺ.	rlbiij. ℥. q. j. ꝺ.
xb.℥.	xj. ℥.	xxij. ℥.	xj. ℥. q. ob.	xrrb. ℥. ij. q. iij. ꝺ.	xbi. ℥. ij. q. iij. ꝺ.	rrriij. ℥. ij. q. j. ꝺ.	xlbj. ℥. ꝺi. ij. ꝺ.
xb.℥.bi.ꝺ.	x. ℥. ꝺi. iiij. ꝺ.	xxi. ℥. q. j. ꝺ.	x. ℥. iij. q. iij. ꝺ.	rrj. ℥. iij. q. j. ꝺ.	xbj. ℥. q. j. ꝺ.	rriij ℥. ꝺi. ij. ꝺ.	xliiij. ℥. ꝺi. iij. ꝺ.
xbj.℥.	x. ℥. q. ij. ꝺ.	xx. ℥. ꝺi iiij. ꝺ.	x. ℥. ꝺi. j. ꝺ. ob.	rr. ℥. iij. q.	rr. ℥. ij. q. ij. ꝺ.	rrrj. ℥. ꝺi. iiij. ꝺ.	xlij. ℥. q. j. ꝺ.
xbj.℥.bi.ꝺ.	x. ℥.	xx. ℥.	x. ℥. q.	rr. ℥. ꝺi.	rr. ℥. ꝺi. q. ij. ꝺ.	rrr. ℥. ꝺi. iiij. ꝺ.	rlj. ℥.

The assise of bread, newly corrected and enlarged, from twelve pence the quarter of wheat, unto three pound and sixpence the quarter
London, 1600
Shelf mark: STC 874
(illustrated at left)

Bread was the mainstay of most people's diets, whether cut up into sippets and incorporated into a fricassee or a pottage, used as a thickener, or eaten with most other dishes. Many flours were known to Shakespeare and his contemporaries: wheat and rye, rye alone, and barley. William Harrison also wrote about a number of unusual flours that had been used in times of hunger: beans, peas, oats, even acorns and lentils. (Harrison, 133) Manchet bread was called white and was eaten by the gentry. Cheat, called "wheaten," and two sorts of brown bread were more common tablefare for "servants…and the inferior kind of people to feed on." (Harrison, 134) He reports that northern farmers near Kendal were unfamiliar with summer wheat and winter barley, both of which were familiar grains in his part of Essex.

The assize specified the types of bread that could be made: simnel bread (a bread first boiled then baked), white, wheaten, household (brown), and horsebread (a bean and bran flour bread intended for horses). Minimum weights for breads were set in order to prevent adulteration of flour or removal of dough from the unbaked loaf. Making of spice breads, buns, and "biskets" was only allowed for funerals, Good Friday, and Chrismas. Foreign bakers' breads were supposed to weigh two or four ounces more than those of free bakers. To further control production, the assize required that each baker mark his bread with a seal.

> of Cookery. 9
>
> A Table of Direction for a Bill of fare for fifh-dayes, and Fafting-dayes, Ember-weekes, or Lent.
>
> The firft Courfe for the fame dyet.
>
> 1 A Difh of Butter.
> 2 A Rice milke.
> 3 Buttered Egges.
> 4 Stewed Oyfters.
> 5 A boyled Rochet oʒ Gurnet.
> 6 A boyld Sallet of Hearbes, oʒ of Carrets.
> 7 A boyled Pike.
> 8 Buttered Loaues.
> 9 Cheuets of Ling oʒ Stockfifh.
> 10 Another Sallet.
> 11 Stewed Trouts oʒ Smelts.
> 12 A difh of buttered Stockfifh.
> 13 Salt Eele, oʒ white herring.
> 14 A Jole of Ling.
> 15 A Skirret pye.
> 16 Buttered Flounders oʒ plaice.
> 17 An Eele oʒ Carpe pye.
> 18 Haddocke, Frefh Con, oʒ Whiting.
> 19 Salt Salmon.
> 20 A Cuftard.
>   The

John Murrell (fl. 1630)
Murrels two books of cookerie and carving. The fifth time printed
London, 1638
Shelf mark: STC 18303
(illustrated above)

Murrell's cookbook includes "a Bill of Fare for fish-dayes, Fasting-dayes, Ember-weekes or Lent…all set forth according to the new English and French fashions." Dedicated to Martha Hayes, the daughter of London's Lord Mayor, Murrell's collection was first published in 1621. His professional travels in France, Italy, and The Netherlands may have inspired him to publish "by reason of the general ignorance of most men in the practice of catering."

The Lenten menu (part of which is illustrated on the previous page) contains some of the foods more commonly found in the yeoman's diet, as suggested by Joan Thirsk. (Notes, 1997) The "boyld sallett of herbes [vegetables] or of carrets," "buttered parsnips," "tarte of spinnage or carrets," and the buttered eggs resemble the diet that William Harrison ascribed to the poor in 1577. (Palliser, 7) In Yarmouth, carrots and other roots grown initially to feed the poor were exported from the Norwich area to London. Cargoes could be as large as thirty tons. (Thick, in Chartres, 287)

Thomas Tryon (1634–1703)
A new art of brewing beer, ale, and other sorts of liquors
London, 1691
Shelf mark: T3189

Agricultural manuals like Tryon's often featured newly-introduced crops as a mechanism for providing work or food for the poor. In this case, Tryon offers "a good and profitable way for the Poor, and wholsom for the Rich, to make Cherry-wine, or Drink of Gooseberies, Currans, Apricocks and Plums, being easie and wholsome, pleasant and cheap." (Tryon, 91) Tryon gives two recipes, concluding that by using one's own cherries, it will cost "very little more than ordinary Beer, and be much stronger." (Tryon, 93)

Photograph courtesy of the Jamestown-Yorktown Educational Trust.

Costrel
Leather
England, 1600–1700
Jamestown-Yorktown Educational Trust
JY.98.21.1
(illustrated below left)

A costrel is a bottle or flask with a bulbous body, narrow neck, and two handles. Intended to be carried like canteens, costrels were "most used among the shepheards and harvest people of the countrey," according to one early seventeenth-century chronicler. (Chappell, 515)

Leather drinking vessels of all sorts were common in the sixteenth and seventeenth centuries when pottery, glass, and metal containers were rare and expensive. A medieval ballad rejected wood, glass, and silver bottles, concluding that,

> *A leather bottel we know is good,*
> *Far better than glasses or cans of wood,*
> *For when a man's at work in a field,*
> *Your glasses and pots no comfort will yield;*
> *But a good leather bottel standing by,*
> *Will raise his spirits, whenever he's dry.*
> *So I wish his soul in heav'n may dwell*
> *That first devised the leather bottel.* (Chappell, 515)

Penelope Jephson Patrick (b. c1646)
The receipt book
Manuscript, 1671, 1674/75
Shelf mark: V.a. 396
(illustrated above right)

Many of the cookery recipes in this collection have their sources recorded, like the pease pottage "from the Cook in Suffolk-Street." (Patrick, 23) Patrick's recipes show her familiarity with new French cooking fashions. The pease pottage, thickened with "gelly broth" is flavored with clove-studded bacon and with sorrel, spinach, and a little mint. This unusual flavoring combination is also found in La Varenne's *Le Cuisinier François*, 1650. (Marcoux, 8) Some of her other recipes include carrot pudding, a French veal pottage, Chocolate, and "Marmalade of oringos, the Lady Jones way." (Patrick, 58)

Pease pottage from the Cock in Suffolk Street

Take two quarts of pease to two gallons & a half of water. when they are very well boild, strain them through a Cullindar; and if y^u would make a quart of pottage, take almost a pint of the pease broth & add to it as much of strong or gelly broth that hath no thickning in it; and half a pint of new milk. Then take two ounces of bacon & stick 4 cloves into it. shred into it an hand full of sorrel & spinage, with a little Mint. Wⁿ it boils, put into it the gbity of a small egg of sweet butter & half a penny loaf sliced thin. Then season it with a little white pepper beaten small, & some salt. As soon as it boils the first time, put in the bread & butter. when it boils the 2^d time dish it up.

Elizabeth Fowler (fl. 1684)
Cookery book
Manuscript, 1684
Shelf mark: V.a. 468
(illustrated next page)

Fricassees involve frying and baking. The word comes from the French *frire*, to fry, and *casser*, to break. Small pieces of meat were fried, then simmered in broth with seasonings. The broth was thickened and served over sippets. Fowler's "ffrigasy of rabet or chickin" flavored with herbs exemplifies the change away from highly spiced foods that was being adopted in upper class kitchens by the 1680s.

The frequency with which meat was eaten and the amounts consumed seemingly everywhere in England caused much comment among foreign visitors before 1700. As markets and farm regions specialized their wares in the early 1600s, many urban dwellers and gentry experienced a more varied diet that contained abundant meat, fish, dairy products, beer, and wine.

John Archer (fl. 1660–1684)
Every man his own doctor…shewing…how every one may know his own constitution and complexion
London, 1673
Shelf mark: 245012
The gift of Mary P. Massey

Archer's aim was to prevent "the great damage that comes upon most people daily by not knowing. . . thereby many dig their Graves with their Teeth. . . ." (Archer, A2–3) Each chapter in his manual addresses a different component of diet, its humor, uses, and flavors. The cereals that Archer describes are flours: wheat, barley (including spelt), and rye. Recipes include a barley broth that nourishes the sick. Rice boiled in milk makes a pudding-like sweet which "increaseth seed." He describes tobacco as "a new hot bath" that results in a reduced craving for food. (Archer, 42–43, 67) Archer, a court physician, lacked a prominent patron and only wrote one book. His work shares a preoccupation with increasing fertility with that of most of his more accomplished contemporaries.

then take a little water & boyle a quarter of a pound of
currens wth a little sliced nuttmeg simon butter viniger
and the oreng pooll minced: a little shuger & the
Juc of orong so when ye calues head is ready put
it in the dish wth ye Jaws so serue it to the table
garnish ye dish wth oreng peele & salt ————

49 How To make a ffrigasy of rabᵗ or chickin

Take them and skin them both and bruse
them in pices wth a knife take good store of
onions and parsly broad time and winter sauory
Chop them very small and set them in a frying
pan wth water till they bee tender then put in
the meat being cut in pices and hancht with
a knife and when ye meat is tender tak it
up and the herbs and Lett the water run
through a rang then put half a pound of bute
into the frying pan when the water is cleane
from the water put them & herbs bak into
the pan fry it very weell wth the butter

then take 3 egg and halff a pinte of creme
beat them toogether very weell with flicced nut
meg and salt stir it into a deep dish with
six oth in a Little whitwine then fry oysters dipt
in eggs you must lett ye meat fry till it is broun
and a little metmeg beat wth your eggs lay
it upon top of ye meat clarrified in eggs
garnish the dish wth some of the sam or barberi or
or flowers

Boyle youre calues head very tender &
cut it in slices cleare from all the bones &
saue the grauy take a pinte of whitwin
& put in the grauy and put it on a Chefin
dish of coales and lett it stew half an hour
then put in the braines wth a handfull off
Capours wth hole pepper salt & sliced nut
megg. haf a pound of butter keep stire my
it till the butter is melted then serue it
to the table on sippets garnish youre
dish with Barberies

Cloues the pound	iiij.s.	£ 22 : 8 : —
Maces the pound	v.s.	£ 28 : — : —
Nutmegs the pound	ij.s.vj.d.	£ 14 : — : —
Cinamon the pound	iij.s.iiij.d.	£ 28 : 13 : 4
Pepper the pound	xx.d.	£ 9 : 6 : 8
Ginger the pound	vj.d.	£ 2 : 16 : —

smirna or raisins 18 ʒ'lond

Almonds the C. waight, cont. 112.pound	xl.s. *the pound q⁰ ¼*
Dates the C. waight, cõt. 112. pound	xl.s.
Liquerise the C. waight, cont. 112. pound	x.s. *q⁰ ¼*
Currants the C. waight, cont. 112. pound	xxx.s. *q⁰ ¼*

wares, voc.
Grocery {

Reisins {
- Great the peece — x.s.
- great the hūdred waight, cont. 112. pound — xiij.s.iiij.d.
- of the Sun the C. waight, cont. 112.pound — xviij.s.

Prunes the C. waight, cont. 112.pound — x.s.

Anniseedes the C.waight, cont. 112. pound — xxx.s. *q⁰ ¼*

Figgs {
- the topnet, cont. thirty pound — ij.s.vj.d.
- the peece, cont. sixty pound — v.s.
- the C. waight, containing 112. pound — xvj.s.viij.d

Sugar

James I
*The booke of rates for the valuation of merchandizes
and collection of our customes. . .within. . .Ireland*
London, 1624
Shelf mark: STC 7695.5
(illustrated at left)

These rates present an increase over the earlier 1613
rates imposed by James I. Special increases were provided for "Cowes, Heiffers, and Steeres alive: Wool,
Yarne, Tallow, Butter, Herring, Pilchers, and Rugges"
shipped from Ireland into England or other foreign
countries. (Rates, 10) The spices that form the core
flavors in early modern European cooking are listed
as "wares—[called] Grocery." Cloves, mace, nutmegs,
cinnamon, ginger, and pepper were first imported
with the return of the Crusaders around 1250. (Trager,
61) This palate of sweet and spicy flavors was comple-
mented by dried fruit (figs, currants, raisins, prunes)
and verjuice, a tart, acidic juice made from young
grapes or apples. Cooking methods introduced by
La Varenne and other mid-seventeenth-century cooks
emphasize salty/acidic flavors rather than sweet/spicy
ones. (Marcoux, 8) "Graines" were important medicinal plants from West Africa resembling cardamom
and were used to treat fevers and shaking fits. (Gerard,
1542; Hess, 403) While Irish farmers supplied meat
and dairy produce to England, their spices were
imported from England.

M. B. (fl. 1655)
*The ladies cabinet enlarged and opened containing
rare secrets and rich ornaments of several kinds, and
different uses*
London, 1655
Shelf mark: B135.2

This collection of recipes includes three general head-
ings: preserving, conserving, and candying; physick
and surgery; and cookery and housewifery. A recipe
for a gooseberry foole included among the "experiments in Cookery and housewifery" follows a series
of "salletts or sawce." Used in medicinal cookery and
as a luxury ingredient in many prepared foods, sugar
was a familiar flavor to many well-to-do urban
dwellers by 1655. Gooseberry recipes for sweetmeats—
cakes (see Sarah Longe's Receipt book, below), preserves, creams, and fooles—are common, and this
collection also includes a gooseberry stuffing recipe.
The earliest mention of gooseberries in the *Oxford
English Dictionary* dates to 1532, and perhaps the term
comes from a corruption of the French *groseille*, or
currant. (Hess, 261) A foole was usually a dish combining pureed fruit with custard, nowadays called
a trifle. (Hess, 132) Additional recipes in *The ladies
cabinet enlarged* include those for waters and oils
attributed to Lord Ruthven. This "learned chymist"
has not been identified.

Sarah Longe (fl. 1610)
Mrs. Sarah Longe her Receipt Booke
Manuscript, c1610
Shelf mark: V.a. 425

Like many recipe books compiled for home use, Sarah
Longe's manuscript combines three types of recipes:
"preserves & conserves," "Cokery," and "Physicke &
Chirurgery." Her recipes for "Cakes of Gooseberies,"
"Cherrie Marmelet," Sugar Cakes, and "Biskets" make
it clear that sugar was a favored ingredient. Cherries,
according to Gerard, were often used for sweet tarts
and as a distilled water to prevent "falling sickness."
He lists twelve types of cherry trees, noting that the
black cherry grows wild in Kent, and in the North of

Pimienta negra.

England, near Westmorland, and at Lancashire "almost in every hedge." (Gerard, 1502–1507) Marmalade probably came to England as a quince preserve (from the Portuguese *marmelo*) in the early sixteenth century. Many recipes present the finished, brightly colored sweet boxed, as does Longe. (Hess, 232–236) During the winter season, such colored condiments provided visual appeal to the meal. A complete transcription of Longe's book starts on p. 102.

Lady Mary (Vanlore) Powell (d. 1651)
Letter, 10 November, 1630, to her and her husband, Sir Edward Powell, bart. (c1580–1653) from their stewards, Thomas Crompton and Jonathan Beale
Manuscript, 1630
Shelf mark: X.c. 51 (19)

Crompton spent much of his time procuring food for the Powell's country household and staff in Weston Zoyland, Somersetshire. He complains that "sault is exceeding deere at Bridgewater [Market]. Ba[y]sault at 15 *l*: & 16 *l* a busshell." Crompton sent a man to Bristol who paid 5 *l*: 8*d* a bushell, enough he writes for "betweene this and Ester." Freshly butchered meat was salted in late fall for winter consumption; thus Crompton needed large amounts of good quality salt in order to insure that the cured meats would not spoil. William Harrison claimed in 1577 that white (table) salt and bay salt (for preserving) were made in England near Scotland and in Essex. (Harrison, 375–378) Bay salt forms from evaporating sea water, as at Nantwich, Cheshire. These salt pans were set up as improvement projects to reduce England's reliance on foreign wares. Salt was also imported from France, where its manufacture was controlled by the state.

Nicholas Webster (fl. 1650)
Certain profitable and well experienced collections for making conserve of fruits
Manuscript, c1650
Shelf mark: V.a. 364

By 1650, the blending of baked meat recipes with fruit recipes would have been familiar to many cooks who compiled their own recipe collections. Locally-grown fruits were traditionally used as sauces. Webster's "baked meat of chicken" combines gooseberries, grapes, or barberries with sugar, cinnamon, and ginger, a flavor combination used with baked meats for over one hundred years. In contrast, recipes for deer, their humballs, and calves' feet call for rosemary and other herbs for flavor.

Christoval Acosta (1515–1580)
Tractado de los drogas
Burgos, 1578
Shelf mark: Massey 1q
The Gift of Mary P. Massey
(illustrated at left)

Herbals and medicinal tracts were published in Latin, French, Spanish, and English in the sixteenth century. Many of them describe new plants found in the Americas and the Indies. Portuguese physician and explorer Garcia de Orta reached Goa, capital of Portuguese India, in 1534. In 1563 he published a colloquy about Indian medicines. Acosta's work repeats de Orta's text adding illustrations of plants. Both works were translated into Latin by Nicolas Monardes and de l'Ecluse. Gerard claimed that pepper (*Piper nigrum*) "is good to be put in medicaments for the eyes." (Gerard, 1540) About thirty years later Sarah Longe used a pennyworth of both black and white pepper in her recipe "for expulsion of wind." (Longe, 37)

Jan van der Straet (1523–1605)
Saccharum in *Nova reperta*
Antwerp, c1600
Engraved by Jan Galle
Shelf mark: Art vol. f81, plate 13
(illustrated next page top)

SACCHARVM.

Qua Saccharum paretur arte, plurimis   Pictura, quam vides, docebit te modis.

OLEVM OLIVARVM.

Decuſſæ oliuæ adhuc acerbæ, ex arbore,   Preſſæǫ, pinguis dant oliui copiam.

Van der Straet depicted the new discoveries of America and the West and East Indies in popular engravings, some of which showed how New World products like sugar were processed for use. The artist has minimized the intense labor needed to produce what was becoming, by 1600, a popular luxury for elite Europeans.

Jan van der Straet (1523–1605)
Oleum Olivarum in *Nova reperta*
Antwerp, c1600
Engraved by Jan Galle
Shelf mark: Art vol. f81, plate 12
(illustrated below left)

Olive oil is recommended by Gerard as a dressing for raw artichokes. The earliest English example of an olive oil and vinegar dressing for a raw, green salad appears in 1390 in *The Forme of Curry*. (Hess, 15)

James I
Proclamation prohibiting the importation of pepper from forraine parts by any other persons than those of the East Indian Company
London, 1609
2 broadsheets
Shelf mark: STC 8442

Chartered December 31, 1600, the Honorable East India Company initially made annual voyages to the Indies around the Cape of Good Hope. The merchants challenged the Dutch-dominated spice and pepper trade. In 1603, the first English ships returned to port carrying cargoes of over one million pounds of pepper. (Trager, 111)

Spice Cabinet
Wood
England, 17th century
Collection of George Way

Red streak

Vinetum Britannicum:
OR A
TREATISE
OF
CIDER;

And other Wines and Drinks extracted
from Fruits Growing in this Kingdom.

With the Method of Propagating all
sorts of Vinous FRUIT-TREES.

And a DESCRIPTION of the New-Invented
INGENIO or MILL,
For the more expeditious making of *CIDER*.

And also the right way of making
METHEGLIN and BIRCH-WINE.

The Second Impression, much Enlarged.

To which is added, A Discourse teach-
ing the best way of Improving BEES.

With Copper Plates.

By *J. Worlidge*. Gent.

LONDON,
Printed for *Thomas Dring*, over against the Inner-Tem-
ple-gate; and *Thomas Burrel*, at the Golden-ball under
Dunstan's Church in *Fleet-street*. 1678.

"A POT OF GOOD DOUBLE-BEER"

SHAKESPEARE, *II HENRY VI* (2.3)

John Worlidge (fl. 1669–1698)

Vinetum Britannicum: or a treatise of cider and other wines and drinks extracted from fruits growing in this kingdom

London, 1678

Shelf mark: 145520

(illustrated at left)

Orchard planting was among the many agricultural projects proposed by reformers like Worlidge. Cider (fermented apple juice), pear cider (perry), metheglin (fermented honey and water, plus herbs) were all easily made, especially in Kent, where fruit trees had been planted abundantly. Harrison lists apple, pear, plum, walnut, and filbert orchards as having been planted in his memory. (Harrison, 269) Cider made from winter or hard fruits was thought to keep the longest. (Best, 209) Worlidge's works are the first large-scale compilations of agricultural literature and draw on writings by Walter Blith, Hugh Plat, and Samuel Hartlib.

Thomas Tryon (1634–1703)

The good housewife made a doctor: or healths choice and sure friend

London, c1690

Shelf mark: T3180

Thomas Tryon considered milk "an incomparable Food and being joyned or mixt with Bread or the Flower of Wheat, hath the first place in all Victuals and is a foundation to all good nourishment." He reasons that because milk is "the emblem of innocence," it is naturally the most desired food of all young beings and will help the sick to recover their strength. (Tryon, 22–23) To this end, Tryon counsels drinking it with baked bread, perhaps sweetened with "good white sugar," up to three times daily. This treatment could be continued as needed for up to a year. Milk pottage thickened with a spoonful of flour for each pint of milk also helped promote "good blood and spirits." (Tryon, 25)

Dairy products were eaten as substitutes for meat during Lent and on fast days. Some authors commended hard cheeses called "bang" as food for the poor. (Kerridge, 86) William Harrison commented that he disliked the flavor of ewe's milk cheese and preferred instead goat's milk and cow's milk cheeses. (Harrison, 311) Devon farmers supplied these "white meats" to London markets.

Gervase Markham (1568?–1637)

The English housewife

London, 1631

Shelf mark: STC 17353

Markham illustrated the gauging marks that helped the housewife to identify her wines. Sweet wines were preferred, although most table wine was served watered. Markham also guided the housewife through the work of choosing, clarifying, extending, and preserving many varieties of wine. The "remedy for claret, or white wine that drinks foul" involves paring and adding a dozen new pippins, which gives "a good scent at the nose." (Best, 144) While the housewife's improvements to her casks, such as skim milk and egg whites, may seem unusual to us, many modern vintners add albumen (egg white) and cassein (skim milk) to their wines. Numerous recipes in this book call for large quantities such as a tun (252 gallons), although others call only for a sestern (about three or four gallons).

William Y-Worth

Cerevisarii comes: or, the new and true art of brewing
London, 1692
Shelf mark: Y216

Most families quenched their thirsts with either weak ale or beer. When William Harrison described ale, in 1587, as "old and sick men's drink," he was making note of how drinking habits had changed. (Harrison, 139) Hops had been introduced to England in the 1520s, and Mistress Harrison and her maidservants brewed once a month using a recipe flavored with bayberries, orris, and long pepper. (Harrison, 137–139)

Ales were brewed with malt and water while beer contained hops, which imparted a bitter flavor. Y-Worth's goal was improved durability for long voyages, and he recommended adding "Burning Spirit" during fermentation in order to prevent souring. (Y-Worth, 108) Consumption of weak, low-alcohol drinks in England at this time has been estimated at around one gallon per person per day. (Hess, 17)

Gallobelgicus (pseud.)

Wine, beere, ale, and tobacco.
Contending for superiority
London, 1630
Shelf mark: STC 11542
(illustrated at right)

The complementary pairs of sweet flavors (wine and sugar) and bitter/spicy flavors (beer and nutmeg) found in this dialogue are similar to those found in cooked dishes. Additives to wine and beer were considered improvements and preservatives.

Company of Distillers of London

The Distiller of London. Compiled and set forth by the special license and command of the King's most excellent Majesty, for the sole use of the Company of Distillers of London. And by them to be duly observed and practiced
London, 1698
Shelf mark: 248662
The Mary and Eric Weinmann Acquisitions Fund

These rules address production of distilled "high spirits, Strong-waters, or aqua vitae," and set basic strengths and proper names to be used by all freemen of the company. (Distiller, 14) Makers were required to identify themselves by marking their wares. Concerns about the addition of musty beer dregs or rotten fruits and spices to spirits indicate some of the dishonest practices then current. Recipes for strong proof spirits combine the spirit with an herb or spice and end with the direction, "dulcify with white sugar." Garden herbs like balsam, lavender, marjoram, rosemary, and sage were all distilled and used to balance patients' humors. The process of distillation was thought to concentrate humors of the plant. (Best, xli)

THE SPEAKERS.

WINE, *A Gentleman.*

SVGAR, *His Page.*

BEERE, *A Citizen.*

NVTMEG, *His Prentice.*

ALE, *A Countrey-man.*

TOST, *One of his rurall Seruants.*

WATER, *A Parson.*

TOBACCO, *A swaggering Gentleman.*

WINE,

VVINE, BEERE,
ALE, and
TOBACCO,

Contending for Superiority.

Sugar and Nutmegge from seuerall doores meete.

Sugar.   *Vtmegge?*

Nut. Sugar? well met, how chance you waite not vpon your Maister, where's Wine now?

Sug. Oh sometimes without Sugar, all the while he's well if I bee in his company, tis but for fashion sake, I waite vpon him into a roome now and then, but am not regarded : marrie when hee is ill, hee makes much of mee, who but Sugar? but to my remembrance I haue not beene in his presence this fortnight, I hope short-ly hee will not know me, though he meete me in his drinke.

Nut. Thou hast a sweete life in the meane time Sugar.

Sug. But thou art tied to more attendance Nutmegge vp-on your Maister Beere.

Nut. Faith no, I am free now and then, though I bee his Prentice still, Nutmegge hath more friends to trust to then Beere : I can be welcome to wine thy master sometimes, and to the honest Countrey man Ale too, But now I talke of Ale, when didst see his man prethee ?

Sug.

49

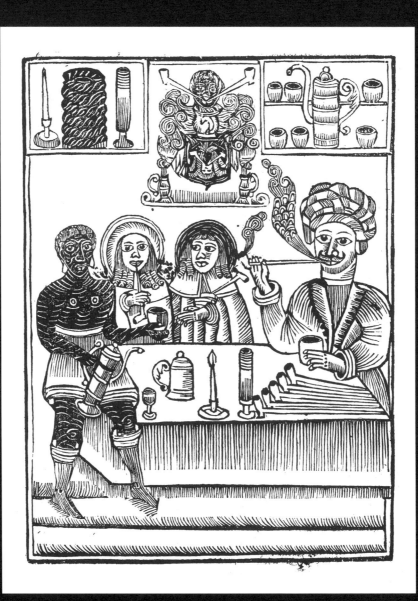

A broad-side against coffee
Published with James I's
Two broadsides against tobacco
London, 1672
Shelf mark: J147
(illustrated at left)

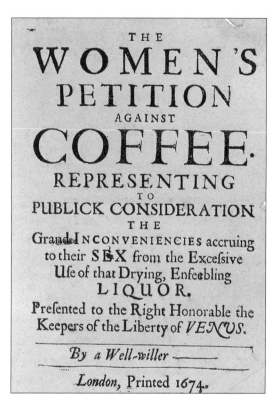

This anonymous poem contains what may be the earliest English illustration of a coffee-house. The poem contrasts Coffee as a medicine, or "Physick," with distilled waters. Like sugar and similar luxuries, coffee was introduced to England for its medical properties. Coffee is described as "cold as earth" and "Ver boon for de stomach, de Cough, de Phisick[!]." The hot temperature of the drink seems to be its chief virtue, for the author recommends it to cure drunkenness, concluding that "a Dish of Broth, or Beer, will work the same cure, if it be drank as hot."

In 1580, a German traveler to the Ottoman Empire described the custom there "of drinking a good beverage called *chaube* as black as ink and very useful in the case of stomach infirmities." Coffee did not become widely available, however, until after 1651, when the first English coffee-house was established at Oxford, and when coffee's bitter flavor could be sweetened with refined sugar. (Brown, 7–11)

The women's petition against coffee. Representing to publick consideration the grand inconveniencies accruing to their sex from the excessive use of that drying, enfeebling liquor
London, 1674
Shelf mark: W3331
(illustrated above right)

Coffee had a reputation in medical circles for preventing drowsiness, but it was also considered so drying

that the result was impotence. Other grievances outlined by the author of this pamphlet include the worry that men "like so many frogs in a puddle, they sup muddy water, and murmur insignificant notes till half a dozen of them out-babble an equal number of us at a Gossipping." (Petition, 4) The author characterizes the coffee-house as "a pimp to a tavern" where men can be drunk three times daily. She describes the usual dose of "Settle-brain" and tobacco taken together as two dishes and two pipes. (Petition, 4, 5)

The mens answer to the womens petition against coffee, vindicating their own performances
London, 1674
Shelf mark: M1721

In response to *The women's petition*, this author defends the coffee-house as "the Citizens Academy," where coffee "both keeps us sober and can make us so." (Answer, 5) His defense of male performance illustrates the prevalent association of certain foods with love. Spiced meats, anchovies, cullises (strong meat broths), jelly-broths, lambstones (kidneys), and bolonia sausages are all part of his list of aphrodisiacs. (Answer, 2) He sends the wives to bed alone with only bonny claber (partly churned, thickened sour milk) to drink.

Henry Stubbe (1632–1676)
The Indian Nectar, or a discourse concerning chocolata: wherein the nature of the cacao-nut. . .is examined
London, 1662
Inscribed on the title page: "T. Willughby"
Possibly the Willoughby Family
(Wollaton Hall) copy
Shelf mark: S6049
The Gift of Mrs. John Moors Cabot
(illustrated above)

TRAITE'
DU
HOCOLATE.

CHAPITRE I.

e c'est que le Chocolate, &
examen des ingrediens
qui le composent.

'USAGE du
Chocolate est
devenu si com-
mun en Euro-
pe, principa-
lement en Es

Stubbe sets forth the medicinal purpose of chocolate: "that muddy Drink, or Ale, with its bitterish taste *satisfies*, and *cools* the body, not intoxicating in any way the Head." (Stubbe, 44) Like coffee, chocolate was considered cold and dry. To make the drink, cacao-nut paste, sugar, and American or Brazil pepper were mixed, then heated in water, and drunk. Other Spanish additions to chocolate included anise seeds and nutmeg, while the English enjoyed their chocolate mixed with milk, spirits, or a claret solution. Stubbe traveled to Jamaica as physician to Lord Thomas Windsor, Governor of Jamaica, in 1662. He writes that he is leaving his own chocolate recipe with a trusted "poor man, Richard Mortimer in Sun-Alley in East Smith-field" should any other physicians wish to use his recipe. (Stubbe, A4–5) His preferred mixture was "not with milk alone...sometimes...1/2 part and dip in a piece of diet-bread or wig [a bun or small cake], etc....or add a spoonful of orange flower water, or if I am faint with business put in a glass of good canary or malage-sack." (Brown, 34)

Philippe Sylvester Dufour (1622–1687)

Traitez nouveaux & curieux du café, du thé, et du chocolate
Lyons, 1685
Shelf mark: TX815 D8 1685 Cage
(*illustrated at left*)

Originally imported to Spain from Mexico, chocolate paste cakes were produced by grinding the cacao-nuts into paste and forming it into shapes. Cast lozenges weighing about two to four ounces each were a popular format, but other shapes could be had, including paper-wrapped cylinders weighing two thirds of a pound. During the long voyage from the Caribbean islands to England, however, the paste sometimes picked up unpleasant odors from other cargoes. (Brown, 29–31) The additional spices recommended in Henry Stubbe's recipe might have neutralized the smell.

Philippe Sylvester Dufour (1622–1687)

The manner of making coffee, tea, and chocolate.
As it is used in most parts of Europe, Asia, Africa,
and America. With their virtues
London, 1685
Shelf mark: D2455
Inscribed "Francis Bernard"; possibly the Trotter
family library copy

Originally called *cha* by the Chinese, tea was first
mentioned by Father Alexander Rhodes in his
accounts of his thirty years as a Jesuit missionary in
the Far East. Dufour comments that the Chinese live
long lives because of their tea drinking, and he recommends tea for its ability to "hinder the gout and
the gravel in the kidneys." (Dufour, 40)

Dufour's recipe for making tea calls for "a dram
of tea to a pint of boiling water." It was to stand for
about seven minutes and then be poured into earthenware or porcelain cups containing a piece of sugar,
or sugar candy, the size of a hazelnut. Alternatively,
the sugar could be held in the mouth as the tea was
sipped as hot as possible. Especially frugal souls, after
exhausting the leaves in tea, could eat the leaves "as
a salad with oil and vinegar." (Brown, 54)

Nicholas de Blegny (1652–1722)

Le bon usage du thé, du caffé, et chocolat pour la preser-
vation & pour la guerison des maladies
Lyons, 1687
Shelf mark: 181632
(illustrated at right)

Two kinds of tea were available to well-to-do English
consumers in the late 1600s: fermented black tea and
unfermented green tea. De Blegny illustrates teapots
made of silver, pewter, and china, commenting that "it
is immaterial what type of vessel is used for the making of tea[;] all that matters is that they are clean and
heat resistant and that their openings are shut by a
firm lid." In 1671 Sir Kenelm Digby's recipe for tea
included eggs and sugar; the beverage was served as
a pick-me-up after the close of business. (Brown, 53)

34 *Le bon usage du Thé.*

p^re figure

2e fig.

4e fig

5e fig.

J.Hair

Pots a preparer le Thé

du Caffé, & du Chocolat. 35

La matiere & la forme des
taſſes à boire le Thé eſt pa-
reillement diverſe & indiffe-
rente ; neanmoins aux Indes
& en Europe , il eſt aſſés ordi-
naire de preferer aux taſſes ou
gobelets d'Argent ou de quel-
que autre metal que ce ſoit,
les chiques de porcelaines ou
de fayance , par cette raiſon
que leur bords ne brulent ja-
mais les doigts , & que la façon de tenir ces chiques paſſe
pour une eſpéce de bienſean-
ce. Ceux de qui cette façon
eſt ignorée la trouveront re-
preſentée à la premiere figure
de ce traité.

Je ne dois pas ômettre de
dire que la teinture du Thé
doit être buë fort chaude, &
même pendant ſa premiere

Spice Mortar
Wood
Continental, 17th century
Agecroft Association
AH1982. 18ab

Thomas Garway (fl. 1650s)
*An exact description of the growth, quality, and vertues
of the leaf tea*
London, c1660
Shelf mark: G282

In 1657 Garway was selling tea, coffee, and "Spanish
chocolata in the cake, from three shillings to ten
shillings the pound weight" in Exchange Alley.
Referring his patrons to Lovel's *Herbal* and Father
Alexander of Rhodes, Garway enumerated the virtues
of tea. When prepared and drunk with milk and
water, tea strengthened the inward parts and removed
pains from the bowells.

Wenceslaus Hollar (1607–1677)
The Long View of London
Amsterdam, 1647
Shelf mark: Map L85c, no. 29, pt. 2

London's imported luxuries like tea, chocolate, coffee,
and spices originated in the Caribbean West Indies
and the Malaysian East Indies. With the establishment
of the East India Company in 1600, English merchants
could trade directly for spices and tea. Grocery wares
(spices) were sold at Cheapside market along with
flowers, herbs, and seeds. (Alley, 90)

Wenceslaus Hollar's view of London and the
Thames illustrates the large numbers of ships traveling into and out of the city. The little figures hovering
in the sky above represent the parts of the world with
which London traded.

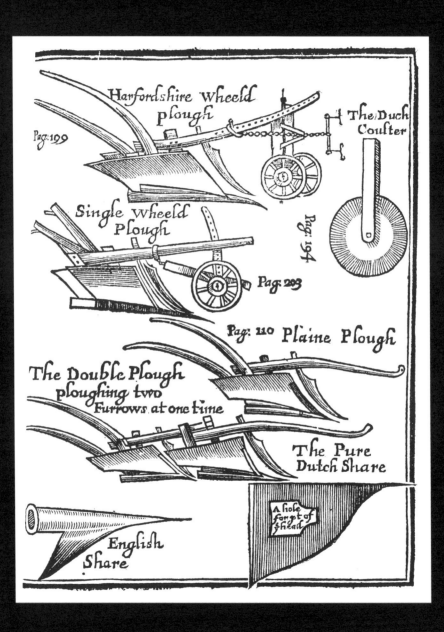

Harfordshire Wheeld
plough

The Duch
Coulter

Pag: 199

Single Wheeld
Plough

Pag: 194

Pag: 203

Pag: 110 Plaine Plough

The Double Plough
ploughing two
Furrows at one time

The Pure
Dutch Share

A hole
for pt of
ye head

English
Share

Walter Blith (fl. 1649)
The English improver improved; or,
The survey of husbandry surveyed
London, 1652
Shelf mark: B3195 c.2
Wilbraham family library copy
(illustrated at left)

Blith's survey, a genre popular in England after the 1550s, focused on ways to improve agricultural practice. Some of his innovations, particularly those concerned with plow blades and shapes, were derived from the practical experiences of Dutch farmers harrowing heavy clay soils. Revived interest in Varro and Columella was strong among rural gentry who sought to improve their lands and maintain the social order. In 1601, Robert Cecil expressed his interest before the House of Commons, saying, "whosoever does not maintain the Plough destroys this Kingdom." (McRae, 35–36)

The improvements presented in Blith's text show the beginnings of specialized farming with techniques and crops particular to certain soils. Reclamation of land came with improved tools and alternative crops and with changing land usage to create more arable fields. Blith deals with irrigating land, draining marshes, enclosing fields, increasing tillage and pasturage, use of manures, and growth of woodlands. New animal fodder such as clover, dyers' woad and madder, brewers' hops, orchard and garden fruits, saffron and licorice, and hemp, flax, and rape (canola) for textiles are all described for their benefits to industrious farmers.

Among the plows Blith describes are both horse- and ox-drawn types. The double-wheeled plows from Hertfordshire are one example of adapting a particular harrow to flinty, hard soils. Another variety, the turn-wheel plow, also called a Kentish plow, was heavy and clumsy and required great strength to use. (Blith, 201)

Thomas Fella
A book of diverse devices
Manuscript, 1585–1598, 1622
Shelf mark: V.a. 311
(illustrated below)

Windmills like the one in Hallisworth, Suffolk, were used to grind grain into the many flours described in William Harrison's commentary on breads. Fella, who was probably from Suffolk, also recorded numerous other scenes of rural life, including harrowing, harvesting, and butchering.

Thomas Tusser (1524?–1580)

Five hundred pointes of good husbandrie
London, 1580
Shelf mark: STC 24380

Tusser's verses made the yearly chores of yeoman farmers and their housewives easy to remember and enjoyed great popularity with middling folk. Expanded from an original one hundred points, Tusser's work remained in print through the eighteenth century. Proper diet, the properties of hops, herbs, and bees, and medicines for sheep and cattle are all included. The abstract for March reminds farmers of planting times for over thirty vegetables and salad herbs, including white and yellow beets, colewort, English and French saffron, and leeks (which he uses for pottage with peas), and lettuce.

Lady Mary (Vanlore) Powell (d. 1651)

Letters mainly to her and her husband, Sir Edward Powell, bart. (c1580–1653), from their stewards, Thomas Crompton and Jonathan Beale
Manuscripts, 1630–1633
Shelf mark: X.c. 51(1)

Bean crops were primarily used as livestock fodder, although William Harrison does mention the use of bean flour for bread when other flour was scarce, and kidney beans were used in cooking. (Palliser, 194) Providing enough hay, straw, and grain for farm animals during the winter was as important a job for Crompton as feeding the household. Describing seasonal threshing work to his employer, Crompton writes that "I have six threshers at worke, four in the Barley Barns one in the Beane Barn & one in the Wheat barn." All of this work filled several farm buildings with "roomes of beanes…and a little barn-full of wheat, the barn being five rooms." While cattle and corn are costly at the nearby market in Bridge-water, grain is plentiful, and he can only sell six bushels of grain a day.

Matthew Stevenson (d. 1684)

The Twelve Moneths, or, A pleasant and profitable discourse of every action, whether of labour, or recreation, proper to each particular moneth, branched into directions relating to husbandry, as plowing, sowing, gardening, planting. . .Lastly every moneth is shut up with an epigrame, with the fairs of every month

London, 1661

Shelf mark: 233515

(illustrated at left)

August labors included grain harvests, cider and perry making, and seed gathering for winter lettuces and herbs. Moderate diet was counseled, and the avoidance of wine, feasts, and banquets, for cool, temperate refreshments balanced the hot weather and its effects. Stevenson remarked that "a little bread to a great deal of Drink makes the Travellers dinner; the Melon and the Cucumber are now in their season, and Oyl and Vinegar dance attendance to the Sallad-herbs." (Stevenson, 37)

John Worlidge (fl. 1669–1698)

Systema Agriculturae; the mystery of husbandry discovered. Treating of the several new and most advantagious ways of tilling, planting, sowing, manuring, ordering, improving of all sorts of gardens, orchards. . .4th edition

London, 1698

Shelf mark: W3602b

(illustrated at right)

Worlidge's engraved title page shows a farmyard surrounded by well-tilled garden beds and fields. In describing all of the farm activities, he includes propagation, care, and harvesting of each plant. Bees and silk worms are considered advantagious projects, as are new crops like hops, licorice, and saffron. Licorice, grown at Pontefract, Yorkshire, and Godalming, Surrey, was considered profitable, and hops, he says, improve land values, perhaps the reason he gives detailed instructions for planting, watering, and picking them. He also describes the oast house or kiln where the hops are dried. Acknowledging changes in taste and diet, he remarks that garden tillage (herbs and vegetables) had "become a more general Food than formerly. . . ." (Worlidge, 145)

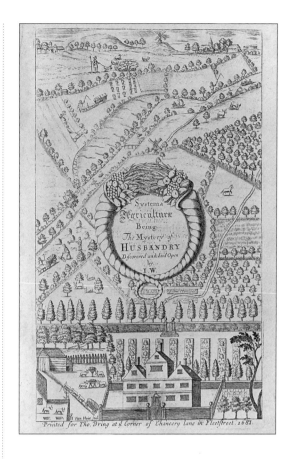

A
NEW ORCHARD
and Garden:

OR

The best way for planting, grafting, and to make
any ground good, for a rich Orchard: Particularly in the North,
and generally for the whole kingdome of England, as in nature,
reason, situation, and all probabilitie, may and doth appeare.

With the Country Housewifes Garden for herbes of common vse, their
vertues, seasons, profits, ornaments, varietie of knots, models for trees, and
plots for the best ordering of Grounds and Walkes.

AS ALSO

The Husbandry of Bees, with their seuerall vses and annoyances, all being the
experience of 48. yeeres labour, and now the second time corrected and
much enlarged, by *William Lawson.*

Whereunto is newly added the Art of propagating Plants, with the true ordering
of all manner of Fruits, in their gathering, carrying home, and preseruation.

Skill and paines bring fruitfull gaines.

Printed at *London* by *I. H.* for ROGER IACKSON, and are to be sold at his
shop, neere Fleet street Conduit. 1623.

William Lawson (fl. 1618)

A new orchard and garden: or the best way for planting, grafting, and to make any ground good, for a rich orchard…as also, the husbandry of bees
London, 1623
Shelf mark: STC 15330
(illustrated at left)

William Lawson drew on forty-eight years of experience tending plants and trees in the North of England to write this guide. He devotes a section of the work to bee husbandry, an important part of household management since honey remained the economical sweetener until the nineteenth century.

William Lawson (fl. 1618)

A new orchard and garden
London, 1618
Shelf mark: STC 15329
(illustrated at right)

This copy of the first edition of Lawson's book was well used by an early owner. In a section on pruning, illustrated to show "the perfect forme of an apple tree," he has marked and underlined instructions on the best time to prune and also the admonition that "if you let them [apple trees] grow great and stubborne, you must do as the trees list. They will not bend but breake."

Nicholas de Bonnefons

The French gardiner, instructing how to cultivate all sorts of fruit-trees
London, 1658
Shelf mark: B3599
(illustrated next page)

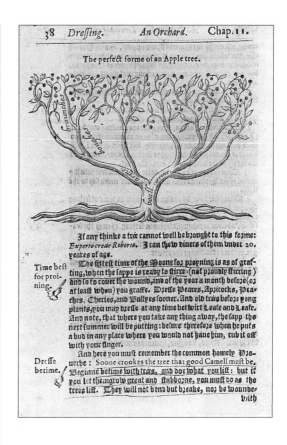

Combining techniques for conserving and drying with instructions on cultivation of garden tillage proved to be a successful formula. Bonnefons' book was printed in one Dutch, one English, and six French editions by 1658. His second treatise describes proper soil and the care of melons, cucumbers, and gourds. Melons were grown in raised beds, four feet long by three feet wide, interplanted with lettuce, chervil, or purslane, and manured with horse dung. Seed sources were very important to Bonnefons, who praises seeds from Italy. He advises gardeners to protect their beds from winds and from theft by enclosing them. His advice is directed at women as melons were thought to excite them.

Thomas Gallen

Gallen, 1666. A new almanack

London, 1666

Tixall Library–Fairfax of Cameron copy

Shelf mark: MS Add 988

(illustrated below left)

Gerard's *Herball* describes apples as "varying infinitely according to the soil and climate," adding that they are a profitable crop whose surplus can be used to feed the poor. (Woodward, 93) He reports that so many kinds grow in Roger Bodnome's Hereford orchards that his servants "drinke for the most part no other drinke but that which is made of Apples." (Woodward, 94)

The owner of this almanac must have taken Gerard's advice to heart. The almanac is interleaved with notes about the orchard at Tixall Hall, Staffordshire. The orchard may have been created from enclosed lands, and it was laid out in four groups of ten trees each. The varieties planted are often named for their place of origin—Holland pippin, Great Bury pear, Flanders cherry. All these crops could have been used to make fermented drinks or could have been preserved in marmalade. Kent, in particular, was famous for its pippins, and recipes for pippin pie are found in many manuscript receipts in the Folger collection.

Franciscus van Sterbeeck (1631–1693)

Citricultura

Antwerp, 1682

Shelf mark: 186422

Oranges were cultivated hot-house fruits and remained an expensive import. Many recipes for orange marmalade used sour Seville oranges, although quince marmalades also appear frequently in lists of sweetmeats. Candied peels, cakes, biscuits, and paste are all orange-flavored recipes found in printed and manuscript cookery books of the period. The bitter flavor balanced the sweet flavors of red wines and spices found in savory pies.

Fruit Trencher
Wood, paint
England, c1700
Jamestown-Yorktown Educational Trust
JS91.22
(illustrated at right)

The word "trencher" evolved from the French verb *trancher*, to cut. In the fifteenth century, sliced, day-old household bread was used as a plate on which to pile food. Everyday trenchers made of wood that did not absorb flavors were widely used throughout society. By 1600, more elaborate, painted versions were made in sets of twelve for use during the banqueting course of the meal where sweetmeats and table fruits were served. The strawberry image on this trencher is accompanied by a verse that may have been read aloud as entertainment.

Strawberries were eaten raw as table fruit, added to tarts, and used to balance the humors. Gerard catalogues three cultivated types: red, green, and white, all of which were small. Distilled strawberry water "drunke with white Wine is good against the passion of the heart, reviving the spirits, and making the heart merry." Ripe fruit was believed to quench thirst and cool the stomach. (Woodward, 138–139)

Photograph courtesy of the Jamestown-Yorktown Educational Trust.

Colander
Lead-glazed earthenware
The Netherlands, 1650–1750
Courtesy of Plimoth Plantation
3.71
(illustrated below)

This colander, made of red earthenware coated with a yellow clay slip, is typical of the inexpensive, utilitarian kitchenware found throughout Europe, England, and America from the fifteenth through the eighteenth centuries.

Randle Holme, in his dictionary of heraldic symbols written in the 1680s, described a "cullander" as

Usefull for a cooke. . .having the bottome full of small round holes: in these Herbs, or such like things are washed, whose dirt and filth runs through the holes, leaving them pure and cleane. (Holme, chap. XIV, 11)

Deep colanders like this one were for draining herbs, fruit, or vegetables, while shallow ones were used for fish. Colanders became increasingly common in the sixteenth and seventeenth centuries as the consumption of fruit and vegetables by people of all social and economic classes increased.

Photograph by Ted Curtin.

The profitable Arte

of Gardening, now the thirde
time set forth : to which is added
much necessarie matter , and a number
of secretes, with the Physicke helpes
beloinging to eche herbe,
and that easly pre=
pared.

To this is annexed tvvo proper treatises,
the one entituled , The maruellous gouernment, propertie, and benefite
of the Bees, with the rare
secrets of the honie
and waxe.
And the other : the yearely coniectures,
meete for husbandmen to knovv :
englished by Thomas Hill
Londoner.

VVherevnto is newly added a treatise
of the Arte of graffing and plan=
ting of trees.

Imprinted at London, by
Henrie Bynneman.

Rims Anno. 1574. *Garth*

Thomas Hill (fl. 1590)

The profitable arte of gardening, now the thirde
time set forth
London, 1574
Shelf mark: STC 13493 c.1
(illustrated at left)

Hill's treatise addresses popular green vegetables
like leeks and artichokes that traditionally had been
considered poor people's food. Randle Holme called
artichokes a "lady's dish meat," meaning that they
were a delicate preparation. Gerard agreed, commenting that the middle pulp and ribs were eaten raw with
pepper and salt. (Woodward, 235) These dishes reflect
the influence of French and Dutch eating habits and
the wider availability of fresh vegetables. Hill recommends sowing seeds for leeks, basil, lettuce, and
endive in a hole together so that "many flavours
and tastes may be felt in one herbe."

Gardening journal

Hastine, Sussex
Manuscript, 1696–1697
Shelf mark: MS Add 933

The gardener who kept this journal carefully recorded
weather conditions and flowering conditions of each
plant, including asparagus, during his second summer
in Sussex. The first asparagus crop was harvested after
three years, if grown from seed; after two if grown
from root stock. Gerard found the vegetable a specialty
of Lincolnshire and that a wild version could be
found in Essex. Evelyn preferred English grown
asparagus rather than the larger Dutch varieties,
although he called all types nourishing. (Evelyn, 20,
41) Also called sparrow-grass, this vegetable was eaten
in boiled salads with a dressing of oil, vinegar, salt,

and pepper, or was pickled to last for a year.
(Woodward, 34–35; Evelyn, 70)

Samuel Hartlib (d. 1662)

A discoverie for division or setting out of land
London, 1653
Shelf mark: H985

Hartlib's work on husbandry (also attributed to
Cressy Dymock) was among the most widely-read
agricultural literature. This plan for draining fen
lands went through five authorized editions in ten
years, and pirated editions were printed as late as
1726. (Ambrosoli, 305–309) A plan for a one hundred
acre farm (see p. 17) shows the house surrounded by
an ordered universe that contains a kitchen garden
for greenstuff, an orchard with a separate garden for
"choice fruits" and one for medicinal plants. Other
areas of housewifely production are given separate
buildings: the dairy, laundry, and bake- and brew-
houses. Closes are allotted to horses and sheep,
and pastures are provided for sick sheep and cattle.
Hartlib repeats the Commonwealth emphasis on
improving the economy and reducing social tensions:

> *For if Husbandry and Trade at home and abroad*
> *be well regulated; all hands may be Employed, and*
> *where all hands are at work, there the whole strength*
> *of a Nation, doth put forth its endevours, for its*
> *own advantage.*

John Worlidge (fl. 1669–1698)

Systema horti-culturae: or, the art of gardening.
Third edition
London, 1688
Shelf mark: 142069

Courtesy of Agecroft Association.

Each of Worlidge's three books elaborates on agricultural improvements: design features, plant care, and kitchen garden foods. Section 1 on the art of gardening outlines recipes for enriched waters for flower trees, artichokes, and asparagus. Standing water is good because it contains bird guano, which acts as a fertilizer. Among the crops listed as food, Worlidge includes roots, peas and beans, cabbages and cauliflowers, melons and cucumbers, and salad herbs. He lists latten and pewter watering pots for use in gardens. Painting with linseed oil and red lead made the pots more durable.

Watering pot
Lead-glazed earthenware
England, 1550–1650
Agecroft Association
AH 1988.1
(illustrated at left)

Made of red earthenware with patches of lead glaze, this watering pot is typical of the utilitarian ceramics made by local potters in England, Europe, and America during the sixteenth and seventeenth centuries. Watering pots had one or two spouts terminating in a large rose with multiple piercings designed, in the words of one early-eighteenth-century writer, "to imitate the Rain falling from the Heavens." (Gentil, 147) Metal watering cans, like one discarded on a Virginia plantation in the 1660s, began to be used in the mid-seventeenth century. (Noel Hume, 68) Irrigation was a challenge to farmers and gardeners alike. Watering pots, limited in size to what a single person could carry, were of practical use only in small kitchen, herb, or flower gardens.

John Evelyn (1620–1706)
Acetaria. A discourse of sallets
London, 1699
Shelf mark: E3480

Evelyn's catalogue of salad plants includes a table of thirty-five different kinds of kitchen garden produce arranged by species. He gives growing instructions, time of harvest, and methods of preparation. The combination of exotics with native plants shows the great variety available by the middle of the seventeenth century. Twenty-five herbs, including lob-lettuce, purslane, Spanish rocket, mustard and turnip greens, fall under the green unblanched category. Nine blanched plants include endive, cabbage, and three lettuces. Edible parts of each plant are also listed, permitting gardeners to enjoy the "tender shoots and tops" rather than the stems. A note adds that young seedling leaves of orange and lemon can be strewn in with the salad in May and June. In July nasturtium flowers may be added.

BILLINGESGATE

FORSTALRS

Hugh Alley (1556–1602)

A caveat for the city of London, or a forewarning of
offences against penal laws
Manuscript, 1598
Shelf mark: V.a. 318
(illustrated above left and right)

Provisioning London's residents required a network
of sixteen markets. Market licenses restricted vendors
to certain times and places. General markets sold sta-
ples like herbs, eggs, butter, cheese, poultry (defined
as live rabbits, pigs, game, and waterfowl), and bacon,
with grain and meal for bread and ale. Billingsgate
sold grain from Thames Valley river ports and from
the Baltic, salt from France, onions and roots, import-

ed oranges and fruit, and fresh/saltwater fish and
shellfish. (Palliser, 318; Archer, 84) By 1546, Leadenhall
vendors provided crops from Essex, Middlesex (corn,
cattle), and Kent (fruit, vegetables, hops), although
most sellers also displayed boars' heads and other cuts
of meat as well as live poultry. (Archer, 88) In 1598,
surveyor John Norden described the housewife's trip
from Middlesex to London:

> *Twice or thrice a weeke [she] conveyeth to London*
> *mylke, butter, cheese, apples, peares, frumentye,*
> *hens, chickens, eggs, baken, and a thousand other*
> *country drugges.* (Palliser, 319)

Several retailing practices irked Alley, who concentrated
on controlling resale of foods in the streets and illegal
private sales in taverns.

Weekly book for a London house
Manuscript, March 25, 1612, to March 25, 1614
Shelf mark: Z.d. 20(1)
(illustrated above)

March 25, called Lady Day, was one of the four quarter
days that divided the calendar. Many household stewards' accounts record quarterly expenses incurred for
food (both cooked and raw), wages, and equipment.
Supplies were bought weekly at local markets or in
September at large fairs like Stourbridge fair near
Cambridge. (Harrison, 395; Palliser, 320)

The names "buttery," "seller," and "pantery" reflect the
foods stored there. Large wine barrels holding about
126 gallons were called butts and were stored in the
buttery. (Best, xliii) The pantry was the storeroom used
for manchet and household breads (from the French
pain, or bread) and baking supplies. In larger households, staffs included servants assigned to each storage
area; hence the butler controlled wine distribution.

These records feature large amounts of meats and
bread, with a few unusual delicacies. The household
prefers sweet wines like claret, bastard (a Spanish
wine sometimes adulterated), and Rhenish wines.
(Hess, 176) Basic cooking fats (fresh and salted, or
preserved butter) are stored in the "seller." Eggs, milk,
and cream used in puddings and custards are among
the fresh dairy produce purchased. Oatmeal was used
to thicken pottages. Calves' feet were boiled down into
jelly and used in stews or as thickener. "Sugar candie"
appears in May, and cherries and strawberries are
among the seasonally available foods listed.

Charles I
The rates of marchandizes
London, 1635
Shelf mark: STC 7695

Saltwater fish and shellfish like oysters, mussels, and
cockles were sold in the streets around Billingsgate
market by fishwives who "cried" their wares. (Archer, 6)
The rates of valuation published under Charles I show
that some varieties of fish were imported. Cod were
caught off of Newfoundland's Grand Banks fishery
and were dried there before being shipped to England.
Before the Reformation, more than one third of the
year consisted of fish days: Lent, every Friday and
Saturday, as well as others, for a total of 153 days.
Fresh fish like salmon, listed in the 1612 accounts of
a London household (above), would have been a welcome change from the more common dried, or salted,
stockfish and whiting. (Harrison, 126) Juan Vives's
Dialogues (1539) include a description of the appropriate sauces for fish: pounded garlic, pepper, mustard.

Aesop

The fables. . .paraphras'd
Second edition, by John Ogilby
Etching by Wenceslaus Hollar
London, 1668
Shelf mark: A697
(see frontispiece)

Storing provisions required dry space that was
rodent-proof. In his illustration for the fable of "The
City Mouse and Country Mouse," Hollar shows
commonly used strategies: egg baskets, barrels,
covered earthenware jugs, hanging meats on nails
and placing pies on shelves. The round pie behind the
mouse is called a coffin. Coffins were an economical
alternative to ceramic pie dishes. The hard crust
(made primarily from rye flour) was not eaten; to
serve the cooked lining one removed the top crust
and scooped out portions to serve to diners. After
the sweet or savory filling was eaten, the coffin
could be re-used. John Shirley's cook book (below)
illustrates coffin shapes used for different fillings.

John Speed (1552?–1629)

Theatrum imperii Magnae Britanniae
London, 1616
Shelf mark: STC 23044

John Speed's atlas of Great Britain was published in
the year of Shakespeare's death. The map of England
not only shows the division of the land into shires but
also some of the inhabitants of town and country. The
country man and woman appear to be provisioning
their house, for he carries a newly caught rabbit and
she a pannier, a basket for provisions. In the upper
right Speed supplies a chart with information about
each county, including the number of market towns.
Specialized regional markets developed as the
improvements recommended by husbandry manuals
became widely practiced and as the need to feed
London became acute. Farmers improved their lands
in response to new ideas and new plants, and crops
like saffron, grown near Saffron Walden in Essex, and
carrots from Great Sandling in Suffolk became available at local markets and fairs.

Cattle and livestock markets were concentrated in
the Midlands, fowl and fish markets near fenland or
the sea, butter and cheese in East Anglia, and grain
markets near rivers of the Eastern counties. (Everitt,
188–191) Navigable rivers, especially in the West,
formed an inexpensive and accessible transportation
network. Approximately 800 markets in England
concentrated inland trade away from smaller villages.
Bristol, for example, dominated trade with Ireland,
receiving fish and hides from Ireland and sending
grocery wares there. Before 1603, trade with Scotland
involved the exchange of fish for English grain at
Lynn and Boston. (Kerridge, 269; Palliser, 323, 328)

si fa lauoreri de latte

neuoue si fa

Luochi freschi doue fu lauoreri de latte

latte mete si fa 4

Bartolomeo Scappi

Opera di M. Bartolomeo Scappi, cuoco secreto di Papa Pio Quinto

Venice, 1605

Shelf mark: TX711 S4 1605 Cage c.2

(illustrated at left)

Although Scappi's dairy and equipment are luxurious, his assistants use the same techniques for turning milk into butter and cheese that were used by English housewives. Milk turned into butter when, during churning, "a sound [that] is light, sharp, and more spirity" was heard in the churn. Between May and September excess butter was potted at large dairies in Holland, Suffolk, and Norfolk, salted for winter use, or sold at markets. In order to produce butter and soft cheeses for market days, the housewife churned on Tuesdays and Fridays. Cream could be kept for up to three days in summer and six in winter. Whey, the liquid that remained after the production of butter or cheese, was often turned into a cool drink seasoned with herbs called "whig," which Markham felt was a good thirst quencher. There were, in fact, so many dairy products being called for that one author commented, "my cow is a commonwealth." (Best, 171–174, xlvi)

John Shirley (fl. 1680–1702)

The accomplished ladies rich closet of rarities . . . Second edition

London, 1687

Shelf mark: S3498A

(illustrated above right)

Shirley writes that "pastry is the most curious part of Cookery." It requires attention. He directs a cookmaid's production of pies in a chapter that teaches

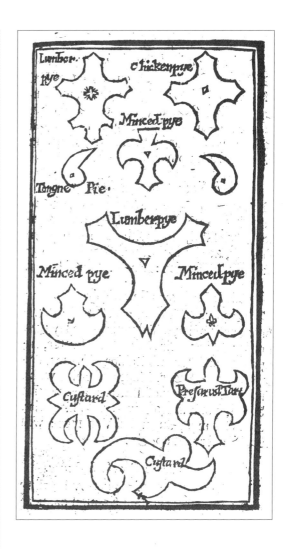

pastry-making and provides twenty recipes. Fillings include fish (oysters, carp, eel), meat and fowl (veal, venison, chicken, sweetbreads, marrow-pudding, turkey, umballs), fruit (wardens, gooseberries, pippins), as well as artichokes, marrow, cheesecake, and custard. For the pastry, flour must be bran free, liquor must be simmered and skimmed, then rosewater or malaga wine added for sweet tarts and custards. For meat pies, the proportion of liquid (which he gives as butter) is one pound of meat to two quarts of liquid, plus new ale yeast or molding eggs "according as you would have your paste light or solid." Necessary tools include "Roaler, Nippers, Spur-iron, Knife, and Plate." Pies were to be flourished or garnished on the lid or sides. The pie shapes appropriate for all the recipes are illustrated. (Shirley, 126–127)

Pies were served with the main course regardless of filling. Crusts were not intended to be eaten but rather to stand up in the oven's heat in place of ceramic dishes. Rye flour was used for "long lasting" dishes, a mixture of rye and wheat for pies that "come to the table more than once." (Best, 97) The air vents cut in the top crust released steam and prevented the pie from exploding in the oven. They also permitted the cook to moisten the filling mixture as necessary. The top crust was lifted off to serve the cooked filling on trenchers.

Susanna Packe

Susanna Packe her booke
Manuscript, 1674
Shelf mark: V.a. 215

Salting was one of the preserving techniques that extended the variety of the winter diet. Packe's recipe for salted eels preserved them for up to three months. Other methods for fish and meats included pickling and sousing in a vinegar bath. (Hess, 75) Among surviving recipes for fruits and vegetables is one that calls for turnips to be packed in trenches and another for peas bottled under butter and salt. To preserve cherries for fresh Christmas tarts, one author recommended storing them in a barrel of hay placed inside a feather mattress. (Hess, 162–163)

Robert May (b. 1588)

The accomplisht cook, or the art & mystery of cookery...the fifth edition
London, 1685
Shelf mark: M1394
(illustrated above right)

Robert May published his cookbook in 1660 after spending fifty-five years cooking for several conservative noble families. His recipes illustrate both the

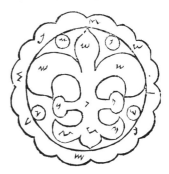

older, medieval style of cookery of May's youth and the new French style that would dominate elite cooking in the eighteenth century. Recent research indicates, surprisingly, that May borrowed few of the one thousand plus recipes he published, in contrast to many of his contemporaries who copied freely from many sources. May's book is the first English cookbook clearly organized in sections without any medicinal recipes. Some of the recipes are accompanied by illustrations that are vivid reminders that food was visual entertainment, whether cut/laid fruit tarts and lobster pies or the brilliant colors of May's green, yellow, and white spinach tart.

Cookeries
Manuscript, late 17th century
Shelf mark: MS Add 752

An almond pottage recipe in this manuscript volume is attributed to "a kook who was five years in [the] king of france kitchin." Although called a pottage, it uses chopped meats (veal, a very good fowl, a pullet) boiled and thickened with pounded almonds, which suggests its French origins. Almonds were used in

European cooking from the thirteenth century onward chiefly as milk or ground and made into marchpane (marzipan). Imported from Spain, almonds were considered an acceptable meat for fast days.

Salt cellar

Tin-glazed earthenware
London, England, 1673
New-York Historical Society
The Gift of Mrs. Nathaniel McLean Sage
(illustrated below)

This molded salt cellar in the form of a seated man holding a basin is one of several surviving examples made between 1655 and 1680 and probably modeled after earlier Flemish examples. (Archer, 325; Grigsby) Salt has always been a valuable commodity, prized as both a preservative and as a seasoning. Its central role in late-medieval and early-modern era cuisine is evident from the elaborate vessels made to hold salt.

©Collection of The New-York Historical Society

Placed to the right of the host or in the center of the table, the salt cellar created a hierarchy of seating with more important diners above and less prominent ones below the salt. Although salt's prominence declined during the seventeenth century, the salt cellar remained an important piece of tableware.

This salt is shaped like a serving man or waiter, a familiar figure among the upper classes of Elizabethan England. A large household staff was considered necessary for people of prominence; Anthony Browne, Second Viscount Montague, had at least six men, in addition to an usher, a carver, and a yeoman of the ewery to wait at table in 1598. (Paston-Williams, 134) Although the average number of servants declined during the seventeenth century, serving men, even ones of clay, were still a sign of wealth and prestige.

A true and perfect inventory of the goodes & chattels of Thomas Betts Late of the parish of Aston in the Countie of Hartford deceased, made and appraised the eleventh day of November in the yeere one thousand six hundred fffiftie eight by John Hatton & John Williams as followeth
Manuscript, 1658
Shelf mark: MS Add 625

When he died in 1658, Thomas Betts left possessions valued at just over £78. From his tools and supplies, however, we can learn something about his eating habits. His dwelling was large enough to include a little chamber, a kitchen, a milk house with loft, a buttery, barn, and shop. His powdering trough was used to salt foods, and the kneading trough for preparing bread dough and pastry for pies. Betts's kitchen equipment—a spit, four kettles, two skillets, and a frying pan—permitted him to roast, fry, sauté, or boil his food. This combination of methods is interesting, as a preference for frying dominated cooking in the south and west of England, while boiling was the preferred method in the north, and baking in East Anglia. (Hacket Fisher, 138) Betts's cow and his cheese-making equipment were highly valued. He may have sent excess cheese from Aston to nearby London markets.

London, Printed for Cha: Adams at the
Talbott in Fleet-ſtreete ouer agt St Dunſtans church

H. Sculp

A ſtewing pan

A towel pan

pl. 6.8

THE
FRENCH COOK

Preſcribing the way of making
ready of all ſorts of Meats, Fiſh and
Fleſh, with the proper Sauces, either
to procure Appetite, or to advance the power
of Digeſtion : with the whole skill
of Paſtry-work.

Together with a Treatiſe of Conſerves,
both dry and liquid, a la mode de France.

The ſecond Edition, carefully examined, and compared with the originall : and
purged throughout, from many miſtakes, and
defects ; and ſupplyed in diverſe things, left
out, in the former impreſſion.

With an Addition of ſome choiſe receits of Cookery lately grown in uſe amongſt
the Nobility and Gentry, by a prime artiſt
of our owne Nation.

Written in French by *Monſieur* De La Varenne,
*Clerk of the Kitchin to the Lord Marqueſſe of
Uxelles, and now Engliſhed by* I. D. G.

London, Printed for *Charles Adams*, at the
Talbut neere St. *Dunſtans* Church in
Fleetſtreet. 1654.

François Pierre de La Varenne (fl. 1651)
*The French cook…the second edition…with an addition
of some choice receits of cookery lately grown in use
amongst the nobility and gentry*
London, 1654
Shelf mark: L625
(illustrated at left)

First published in 1651, La Varenne's cookbook dis-
plays the author's decade of experience as clerk of the
kitchen of the marquis d'Uxcelles. La Varenne broke
with the medieval style of cooking, creating the first
documented roûx liaisons (sauce thickeners) using
flour rather than butter emulsions. The roûx, which
became an important component of French cookery,
could be made in quantity by kitchen boys. La Varenne's
recipe for a "shoulder of wild boar with ragout" features a roûx "stove" (stuffed) with mushrooms and
capers that provided the sharp taste characteristic of
ragouts. Wild boar was eaten from midsummer to
October. (Wheaton, 114–116; Marcoux 8, 16, 51) Alain
Girard estimates that the growing publication of
French cookbooks, such as La Varenne's, between 1650
and 1700 amounted to 75 editions, or 90,000 volumes
in circulation by 1700.

Mary Hookes
Cookery book
Manuscript, late 17th century
Inscribed on the flyleaf, "Mary Hookes, 1680"
Shelf mark: MS Add 931
The Gift of Mr. & Mrs. Alexander H. Jeffries, Jr.;
in honor of Nancy Cutler Fogarty

Thirty years after the publication of La Varenne's
book, Mary Hookes collected a variety of recipes. The

capon larded with lemons in white broth resembles
the boar ragout above.

Jacob Cats (1577–1660)
Proteus ofte minne-beelden
Rotterdam, 1627
Shelf mark: STC 4863.5
(illustrated next page)

Roast meats, particularly beef, dominated English diet
and culture by the late seventeenth century. In 1587,
William Harrison remarked that "there is no restraint
of any meat…in England." (Harrison, 125) Robert
May's cookbook contains few recipes for beef, however.
A New Year's Day menu does include a "sirloin of
roast beef," and May's index lists recipes for pickled
roast beef and roasted beef fillet among six beef
recipes. (May, sigs. b7, b9) The illustration in Cats's
book shows a man in a humble dwelling roasting his
meat (possibly chicken or rabbit) on a spit while a pot
simmers by the side of the fire.

Sir Hugh Plat (1552–1608)
The jewell house of art and nature
London, 1594
Shelf mark: STC 19991 c.1

Plat's life-long interest in agricultural improvement
and his "new Experiments in the Art of Husbandry,
Distillation, and Moulding" show a creative mind
working to improve the food supply. In this little
volume Plat offers ways to preserve meats for up to a
month, regardless of weather, with the goal of reducing waste and improving diets of mariners. The meats
are boiled in strong brine and hung to dry. He claims
that the flavor is not overly salty, and he particularly

Dat sich kan droopen , Is best te koopen.
VIII.

QVam miser iste Coquus, cui nil pinguedinis olla
  Seruat, & assanda est cui male pasta caro!
Non illi grato, redolet nidore culina,
  Splendida non liquido tinguitur offa garo.
Quam miser iste Procus, cui nil habet arca, cuique
  Culta puella domum, sed sine dote, venit!
Ille quidem lætas numerat pro tempore noctes,
  At miseros poterit quis numerare dies?
Ergo puer totis hæc dogmata conde medullis,
  Viuere in dura conditione velis.
Macra foris ne sume, domi si pinguia desint;
  Si bonus esse Coquus, si Procus esse velis.

recommends the recipe for use in hot climates and during the summer months for mutton, veal, and venison.

Hannah Woolley (fl. 1670)

The queen-like closet, or rich cabinet stored with all manner of rare receipts. . . third edition
London, 1675
Shelf mark: W3284

"Kickshaw" and "hash" are Anglicized adaptations of French cooking terms used in the mid-seventeenth century. From *quelquechose* (something), kickshaw came to refer to a puff paste dough filled with "Gooseberries, Raspberries, Curd, Marrow, Sweet-breads, Lambs-Stones, Kidney of Veal, or any other thing what you like best." The thin dough could be eased on molds before being baked or fried and strewn with sugar. (Woolley, 254) Hash describes a common cooking technique (*hacher*, to hack, slice) for sliced meats as well as the resulting dish of meat in stock. Variations appear in May for bullocks' cheeks and many kinds of feet. Flavored with lemon, roasted with claret, whole spices, caraway seeds, rosemary, and salt, hashes were served over toasted manchet bread or sippets. (Hess, 48–49; May, 39)

Bartolomeo Scappi

Opera di M. Bartolomeo Scappi, cuoco secreto di Papa Pio Quinto
Venice, 1605
Shelf mark: TX711 S4 1605 Cage c.1
(illustrated above right)

In this large kitchen used by the Pope's cook, there are several pieces of cooking equipment that were basic to a well-provisioned household kitchen in England. The low wall ovens are topped by clay kettles for simmering and boiling. The hearth is equipped with spits and hanging cranes for large pots. The mortar and pestle in the foreground were essential to any cook preparing sauces or using nuts as thickening or ground spices for flavor. The pasta table, however, marks this kitchen as an Italian one.

Georg Philipp Harsdoerffer (1607–1658)
Vollständiges Trincir-Büchlein handlend
Nuremberg, 1640?
Shelf mark: 223775
(illustrated at left)

While printed bills of fare in cookbooks noted the proper order for serving each course, carving manuals such as this one gave instruction on how to carve in public. Even when households became smaller in the seventeenth century, several servants would have waited on guests during dinner. The carver divided each dish, from baked dishes to sweetmeats. Here the housewife prepares to employ the basic tools necessary: a napkin to cover her arm, a broad carving knife to present food on, and a two-tined fork to hold the meat in place. Presentation of dishes in the correct order by the server was also part of the dining ceremony. The butler dispensed drinks from the tiered cupboard at the rear and served sauces. A basin and ewer was used by each person to wash his hands between the first and second course.

Trencher
Wood, paper
Engraving by Crispijn van de Passe (1595–1612)
England, 1600–1650
Belonged to Edward Winslow of the Plimoth Plantation
Pilgrim Society, Pilgrim Hall Museum No. 149
(illustrated at right)

This trencher is decorated with an image printed on paper that shows one of the farmer's main tasks in November—butchering. The other eleven parts of the set would have been decorated with scenes associated with the other months of the year. The border inscription reads:

November pulls downe hoggs for Bacon Pork and Sowse;
Housewife save for puddings, goode meate in poore
man's howse.

Popular images for decorating trenchers included flowers, moral epigrams, sexual jokes, and husbandry scenes. (de Jongh, 85–89) The roundels were used in banqueting entertainments where the inscriptions were sung or read to other revelers. Large numbers of courtesy manuals were published during the seventeenth century to satisfy the needs of upwardly mobile merchants concerned about how to behave or what to discuss after a meal.

Spoon
Brass
Possibly English, c1600
Collection of George Way

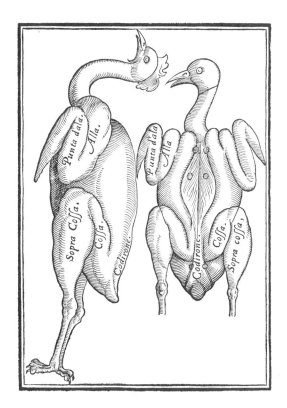

Vincenzo Cervio
Il trinciante
Venice, 1593
Shelf mark: TX885 C4 1593 Cage
(illustrated above)

A variety of roasted birds, puddings, and fricassees
was commonly served in the first two courses of the
midday dinner. The carver performed at a side table
in full view of all guests. He was

> neatly and handsomly to carve it, not touching of it
> so near as he can with his Fingers, but if he chance
> unawares to do so, not to lick his Fingers, but wipe
> them upon a Cloth, or his Napkin, which he hath for
> that purpose; for otherwise it is unhandsom and
> unmannerly…he must be very Gentle and Gallant
> in his Habit, lest he be deemed unfit to attend such
> persons. (Woolley, *Queen-like closet*, 336–337)

Hannah Woolley (fl. 1670)
The accomplish'd ladies delight in preserving, physick,
beautifying, and cookery
London, 1683
Shelf mark: W3271

Several dramatic carving instructions survive in various formats, directing servants or housewives to
"break that goose," "truss that chicken," "unlace that
coney," or otherwise dismember fish, game, and
meats. The constant reprinting of such instructions
may be due, in part, to their vibrant language and
people's interest in antique customs. The commands
may first have been printed by Wynkyn de Worde in
1508. They survive as late as Robert May (1660) and
Randle Holme's *Academy of Armory* (1668), where
they are printed without any instructions for carrying
them out.

Hannah Woolley (fl. 1670)
A guide to ladies, gentlewomen, and maids
London, 1668
Shelf mark: W3278.5

Instructions in this volume detail the proper behavior
of women servants at meals and the guidance their
mistresses should provide. Food was eaten with the
first two fingers and thumb of the left hand. Spoons
were used to eat pie, pottage, and custards, while
knives were used to spear food from one's trencher
and carry it to the mouth. Good table manners were
a mark of respect. (*School of Manners*, 8)

> talk not at all. . .for that is unseemly, unless it be to
> answer your Mistress when she ask you a question.
> Drink to nobody that you think is better than
> yourself. . . . Put not your Knife to your mouth
> unless it be to eat an Egge. (Woolley, 40)

Henry Butts (d. 1632)
Diet's dry dinner: consisting of eight severall courses
London, 1599
Shelf mark: STC 4207
The gift of several donors for the Folger Library's
50th Anniversary

The eight courses in Butts's dinner—fruits, herbs
(vegetables), flesh, fish, whitemeats (dairy products),
spice, sauce, and tobacco—include the basic ingredients in an English diet, except for bread and drink.
His first five categories are foods served at the two

courses making up dinner. His other courses are all seasonings. Butts's meal seems to be designed both as a guide to manners and an herbal, with information about new crops like artichokes and familiar ones like almonds. Each entry is for a specific food and outlines its use, humor, growing patterns, medicinal uses, and the method of cooking it. At the end of each entry is a "story for table-talk" that repeats the history of the food and its sources. These passages may have been used like "posies" on decorated trenchers to entertain diners after a meal.

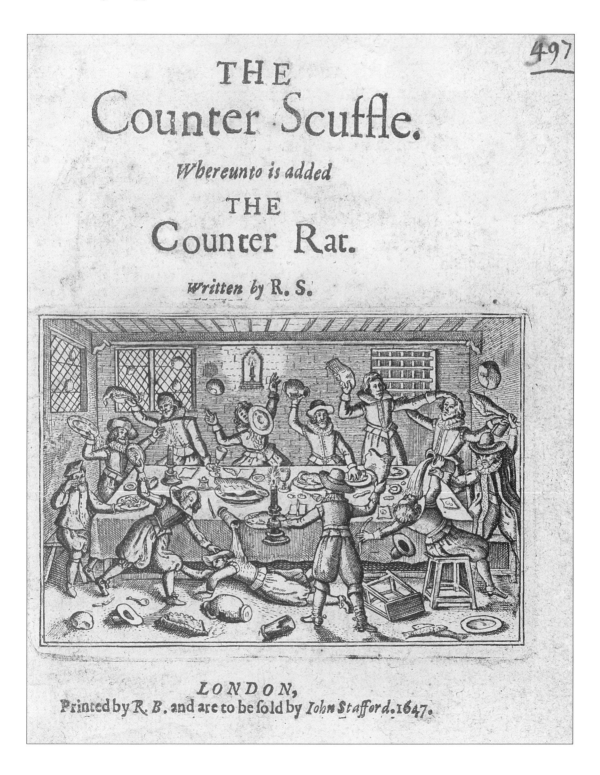

The manner of Placing the Mess on their Majesties Table, being 145 severall dishes, The Figures directed to the Printed Estates shewing what Meats were contained in each Dish. There were 30 dishes more served to their Majesties Table at the second Course.

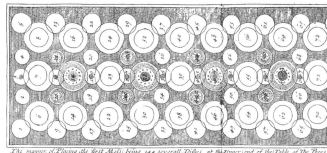

The manner of Placing the first Mess, being 144 severall Dishes, at the Upper end of the Table of The Peers

A Ground Plott of WESTMINSTER HALL, shewing the
Cupboards, Galleries &c. on the day of the

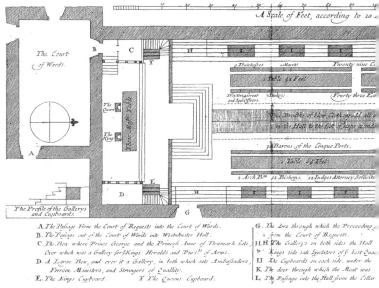

A Scale of Feet, according to 20

The Court of Wards.

The Queen

The King

The Profile of the Galleries and Cupboards.

9 Dutchesses   11 Marchi   Twenty nine

Table 54 Feet

Forty three

Barons of the Cinque Ports.

Table 54 Feet

2 Arch Bps   12 Bishops.   12 Judges Attorney, Solicit

A. The Passage from the Court of Requests into the Court of Wards.
B. The Passage out of the Court of Wards into Westminster Hall.
C. The Box where Prince George and the Princess Anne of Denmark sate
   Over which was a Gallery for y Kings Heralds and Pursts of Arms.
D. A Large Box, and over it a Gallery, in both which sate Ambassadors,
   Forrein Ministers, and Strangers of Quallity.
E. The Kings Cupboard.   F The Queens Cupboard.

G. The dore through which the Proceeding
   from the Court of Requests.
H.H. The Galleries on both sides the Hall
   Kings side sate Spectators of y best Qua
II The Cupboards on each side, under the
K. The dore through which the Meat was
L. The Passage into the Hall from the Cellar

The manner of placing One Mess, being 144 severall Dishes at y upper end of y Table of y Bishops, Judges, and

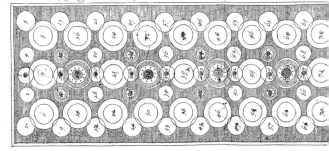

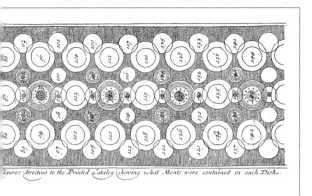

figures directing to the Printed Catalog shewing what Meats were contained in each Dish.

d Dimensions of the severall Tables, Seats,
Coronation. 23 Apr. 1685.

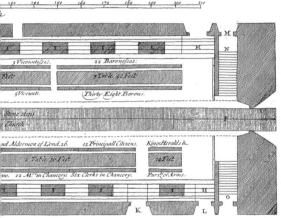

inster Hall
ich on the
sate ♩ Musick
gnor yard.

M. *The Entrance into the Chequer Court where Sweetmeats &c were deposited.*
N. *The Stone Steps leading up to the Court of Exchequer over which was a Gallery for Spectators.*
O. *The Stone steps leading up to severall Offices belonging to the Exchequer over which was a Gallery for Spectators.*
P. *A Portico erected at the Great North dore, leading into the New Palace-yard. Over which was a Gallery for the Trumpetts and Kettle Drums.*

The figures directing to the Printed Catalog, shewing what meats were contained in each Dish

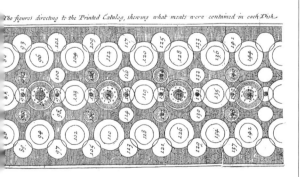

Robert Speed

The Counter Scuffle

London, 1647

Shelf mark: S4890A

(illustrated page 83)

This poem tells the story of a Lenten brawl between a Captain and a Tradesman in a City tavern. The tavern's hospitality did not require the etiquette demanded at formal dinners, nor did entertainment in public houses include genteel table talk.

Francis Sandford (1630–1694)

The history of the coronation of. . .James II. . .and of his royal consort Queen Mary

London, 1687

Shelf mark: 222728

The Gift of Mrs. H. Dunscombe Colt

(illustrated at left)

Among the most elaborate and ceremonial of meals was a coronation banquet. When James II was crowned in 1685, the King and Queen sat enthroned on an elevated dais during the service of 145 dishes in the first course and thirty in the second. Peers and peeresses were served 639 dishes, the archbishops, bishops, barons, judges, 631. In all, the king's master cook, Patrick Lamb, and his staff prepared 1,445 dishes.

The convention was to eat from dishes near your place, not from every one on the table. Trumpets and kettle drums announced each course, music was played from near the Queen, and three galleries of spectators watched the royal family and the assembled clergy, nobility, and officers eat. Clusters of dishes were raised up off the table to create a landscape on the table top.

May hath 31 dayes.

The gladsome shew, that may doth yeeld ✲ Reioyceth all created things ✲
But no reioycing like to that ✲ Which peace of conscience with it brings ✲

Day	breaketh	Sunne	ryseth	Sunne	setteth	The twylight	
houre	miut	houre	minut	houre	minut	houre	minut
2	30	4	23	7	37	10	40

The day is 15 houres and 14 minutes. The night is 8 houres and 46 minut

Ryse early now this month of may ✲ And walke the fields that be so gaye ✲
From surfetting see thou refraine ✲ For fonde it will procure thy paynes

Thomas Trevelyon (b. c1548)
Pictorial commonplace book
Manuscript, 1608
Shelf mark: V.b. 232
The Gift of Lessing J. Rosenwald
(illustrated at left)

The illustration for the month of May in the calendar
section of Trevelyon's commonplace book shows a
garden bower set with ale and sweetmeats for the
lovers. Banqueting "stuffe" was often consumed outside or in specially built houses away from the main
dwelling house, as at Montacute House in Somerset.
A ho-goo, a dish with a particularly fine or piquant
flavor or aroma, might well have been served in such
a banqueting house.

Royal, military, and court costume from the time of
James I
Watercolor miniatures, c1605
Shelf mark: Art vol. c91
(illustrated on cover and above)

In both these scenes servants bring in food or draw
ale and wine for the guests. A roasted fowl, a coffin
pie, joints of meat, a sweet pie, bread, and what may
be a marmalade can be seen on the tables. Trenchers,
knives, and a saltcellar are visible in the dining scene.

Of the place where and how an assembly should be made, in the presence
of a Prince, or some honourable person.

George Turberville (1540?–1610?)

The noble art of venerie or hunting

London, 1611

Shelf mark: STC 24329 c.2

(illustrated at left)

According to William Harrison's account, "beasts of the chase" were deer, fox, and marten. (Harrison, 259) Hunting and falconry were sports of the elite, and venison originally was eaten only by the king.

Turberville's book on the art of hunting illustrates "an assembly. . .in the presence of a Prince, or some honorable person." It is clearly a festive break from, or conclusion to, a hunt. Foods are being removed from baskets and laid out on cloths spread on the ground. A costrel and other containers for beverages are visible in the foreground near the barrels of wine.

Mary Tillinghast (fl. 1678)

Rare and excellent receipts

London, 1690

Shelf mark: T1183

(illustrated above right)

Sugar paste was used for "simple sweetmeat tarts." Tillinghast suggests that her recipes have extra cachet by claiming that they are printed for the use of "her Scholars only." Satires on banqueting contrasted the behavior of the courtiers who ate these delicacies with the simple hospitality of rural gentry. English country foods like "beef puding, and small beare" became subjects of admiration among champions of rural simplicity.

Lobed dish

Tin-glazed earthenware

England or Europe, c1650

Collection of George Way

Grace Randolph

Her booke

Manuscript, 1697

Shelf mark: V.b. 301

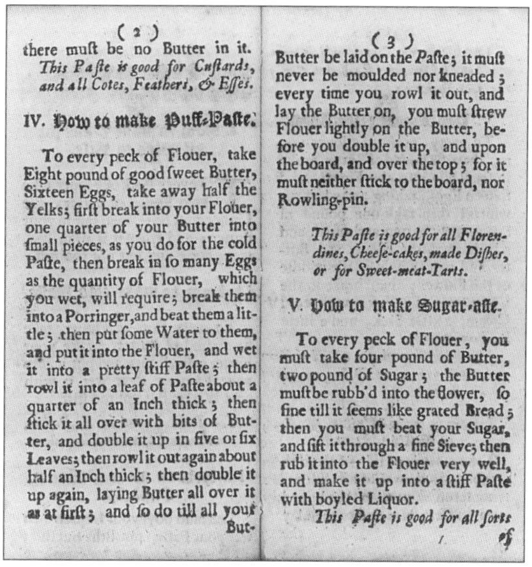

(2)

there muſt be no Butter in it. This Paſte is good for Cuſtards, and all Cotes, Feathers, & Eſſes.

IV. How to make Puff-Paſte.

To every peck of Flouer, take Eight pound of good ſweet Butter, Sixteen Eggs, take away half the Yelks; firſt break into your Flouer, one quarter of your Butter into ſmall pieces, as you do for the cold Paſte, then break in ſo many Eggs as the quantity of Flouer, which you wet, will require; break them into a Porringer, and beat them a little; then put ſome Water to them, and put it into the Flouer, and wet it into a pretty ſtiff Paſte; then rowl it into a leaf of Paſte about a quarter of an Inch thick; then ſtick it all over with bits of Butter, and double it up in five or ſix Leaves; then rowl it out again about half an Inch thick; then double it up again, laying Butter all over it as at firſt; and ſo do till all your But-

(3)

Butter be laid on the Paſte; it muſt never be moulded nor kneaded; every time you rowl it out, and lay the Butter on, you muſt ſtrew Flouer lightly on the Butter, before you double it up, and upon the board, and over the top; for it muſt neither ſtick to the board, nor Rowling-pin.

This Paſte is good for all Florendines, Cheeſe-cakes, made Diſhes, or for Sweet-meat-Tarts.

V. How to make Sugar-aſte.

To every peck of Flouer, you muſt take four pound of Butter, two pound of Sugar; the Butter muſt be rubb'd into the flower, ſo fine till it ſeems like grated Bread; then you muſt beat your Sugar, and ſift it through a fine Sieve; then rub it into the Flouer very well, and make it up into a ſtiff Paſte with boyled Liquor.

This Paſte is good for all ſorts of

Recipes for quince, pippin, and lemon marmalade were popular and were passed on from one cook to another. (Hess, 213, 214) A quince marmalade was "given Queene Mary for a New-year's Gift" and was published over fifty years later in 1608 in *A closet for ladies and gentlewomen, or The art of preserving, conserving, and candying.* (Hess, 235) In Randolph's recipe, four pounds of English cherries are boiled down in sugar. This sweetmeat would have been served in elaborately glazed ceramic or silver or glass dishes.

Behold the maiestie and grace
of loueing, cheerfull, Christmas face.
Whome many thousands with one breath:
Cry out let him be put to death.
Who indeede can neuer die:
So long as man hath memory.

Josiah King

The examination and tryal of old Father Christmas together with his clearing by the jury

London, 1687

Shelf mark: K511.2

(illustrated at left)

Religious aspects of keeping Christmas changed during the seventeenth century, although many farm customs were still practiced. December meant abundant fresh meat for everyone. Wine and beer supplies were ready to drink. In the "Gloucestershire Wassail" (1648), the yeoman singer demands "a bowl of the best" ale and *white* bread as hospitality from his masters. (Nissenbaum, 5–12) While Tusser wrote of seasonal brawn dinners, he also chided those Puritans who

> *Take custom from feasting, what cometh then last:*
> *Where one hath dinner a hundred shall fast.*
> (Rowse, 232)

This book mocks those who would suppress Christmas. The Puritan jury members are all mean, among them Mr. Eat-alone, Mr. Hoord-corne, and Mr. Cold-kitchin, and they are replaced by Mr. Warm-gut, Mr. Neighbour-hood, and Mr. Open-house, who acquit Father Christmas. (King, 8, 15)

A Christmas messe

Manuscript, c1600–1620

Shelf mark: J.a. 1, no. 9

(illustrated next page)

Brawn, made from force-fed boar meat and served with a mustard sauce, is traditionally associated with English Christmas celebrations. Robert May's directions for "set[ting] the meat in order" put brawn dishes first at Christmas and New Year's dinners. The plot of *A christmas messe* involves a battle between the forces of King Brawn and King Beef over who will be served first at the Christmas meal. The cook resolves the debate, and Brawn, assisted by Mustard, is sent in first, followed by Queen Mincepie. (*Messe*, 35, 56) The play was possibly performed at a Cambridge college as an after-dinner lesson in debating style.

Robert Plot (1640–1696)

The natural history of Staffordshire

Oxford, 1686

Shelf mark: 136592

Plot describes how Lord William Paget at Beaudesart coped with his household during the twelve-day Christmas celebration. Paget kept Christmas on his country estate, rather than in London, as many gentry and nobility were encouraged to do from 1596 to 1640 by Royal Proclamation. The household and Paget agreed on basic rules of conduct for the feasting. Transgressors were punished by having their fingers secured into small finger-stocks by the Lord of Misrule. This benign punishment, administered by the figure representing the inversion of normal social order, suggests that the whole affair was a part of the Christmas carnival, expected by the laborers and yeomen and not drastic punishment. (Heal, 119, 273)

Sir Hugh Plat (1552–1608)

Delightes for ladies

London, 1608

Shelf mark: STC 19980

The recipe Plat gives for sugar work creates a walnut made of cinnamon-flavored candy filled with biskets, candied caraway seeds or "a preetie Posey" (i.e., a short song or poem). The mixture of white paste

Enter Belly:

Bel: S't, what's the matter? why doe yee flock soe?
yee thinke belike I'm prologue to soone mockshow.
In this yee neyther wise men are, nor witches;
If yee thinke soe, beleeu't yee wronge your breeches.
For I am come into this goodly hall
To find good cheare & soe I hope I shall.
For wot yee who I am? Belly's my name
A man I'm sure this Christmas in good fame
Wer't not for mee, what would your victualls doe
Euen lye & stink, & mould, & & worse to.
How many Butchers, Bakers, Grosers, all
To Belly to deuoure apace doe call.
If I but once grow queasy, all their ware
Growes streight as cheape as'tis at Bartholmew fare
I'm only in request, for who not wishes,
A Belly correspondent to his dishes?
And now I hope to stuff my gorrell full
This Christmas: But this Cooke this greasy gull,
soe vexeth my poore heart with expectation,
That I could eate him vp without compassion.
well I'le goe call him. why doe yee looke after mee [he lookes
Beleeu't I did not come for you to laugh at mee   back.
                                            Exit:
                    Scena: 2:
            Enter Trencher and Tablecloth:

Tren: Come Tablecloth, heer's such adoe I wisse.
'Twere time ffaith, you had been layde ere this.
Tab: Faire S^r you are as briske as 'twere a wencher,
Ere dinner's done, you'll bee a greasy Trencher.

royal was combined with gum tragacanth (sap from the Persian shrub Astralagus) and rosewater to give it a pliable texture and then molded on a walnut shell. (Hess, 292) Like trenchers, the poem was a banquet entertainment for adults, but Plat also recommended marchpane conceits shaped like pies, birds, baskets. "They bee excellent good to please children." (Plat, 38–39)

Rose Kendall or Ann (Kendall) Crater (fl. 1682)
Cookery and medicinal recipes
Manuscript, c1675–1725
Shelf mark: V.a. 429

Among the recipes collected by women of the Kendall family were those for jumballs and mead. Jumballs were small cookies often shaped into letters. Mead was made with a variety of flavors added to the base of fermented honey. While considered an old-fashioned drink by the late seventeenth century, mead may have had traditional associations with wassail, another drink popular during the twelve days of Christmas.

Thomas Tusser (1524?–1580)
Five hundreth points of good husbandry
London, 1573
Shelf mark: STC 24375

December's good cheer for Tusser's farmer includes brawn pudding along with freshly killed beef, mutton, pork, pig, veal, goose, capon, and turkey. Apples, cheese, and nuts with jolly carols end the "christmas husbandly fare." Tusser's plea for year-round hospitality makes sense in a world where fresh food was available only seasonally and enough to eat depended on a good harvest.

> *At Christmas be merye, & thankful withall,*
> *& feast thy poore neighbors, ye gret with ye small.*
> *Yea al the yeare long to the poor let us geve:*
> *Gods blessing to follow us, whiles we do leve.*
> (Tusser, 30)

For Hannah Woolley's instructions to those who "serve in noble or great houses," see Appendix II, p. 121. The following objects were graciously lent by other institutions or individuals.

Trencher
Wood
England, 16th century
Jamestown-Yorktown Educational Trust
JY98.4.3
(illustrated at right)

Delft jug
Earthenware
England or The Netherlands, c1600
Collection of George Way

Pedestal salt
Redware
London, c1580
Courtesy of Plimoth Plantation
124.88
(illustrated at left)

Borderware pipkin
Earthenware
England, c1580
Courtesy of Plimoth Plantation
92.516
(illustrated at right)

Spoon
Pewter
England, c1600
Courtesy of Plimoth Plantation
2091
(illustrated at right)

Carving Knife
Steel, horn, brass, mother-of-pearl
France, 17th century
Agecroft Association
AH1982.1

Wafer iron
Iron
Probably England, 1623
Collection of Jonathan Z. Friedman

Grand Sallet (reproduction)
Agecroft Association

Photographs courtesy of Plimoth Plantation by Ted Curtin.

By the King.

❧ A Proclamation for reliefe of the poore, and

remedying the high prices of Corne.

HE Kings most Excellent Maiestie, hauing taken knowledge of the present scarcity and dearth, and of the high prices of Corne and graine throughout all parts of this Kingdome, hath beene pleased by his Proclamation lately published, to restraine the residence of the Lords Spirituall and Temporall, and of the Knights, and Gentlemen of quality, in, and neere the Cities of London and Westminster, and other Cities and Townes, and to returne them vnto their owne houses & habitations in their seuerall Countries, that all partes of the Kingdome might finde the fruites, and feele the comfort of their hospitality and good gouernment: wherein, as His Maiestie is well pleased with the dutifull obedience of great numbers, that according to His Royall command, haue left the Cities of London and Westminster, and the parts adiacent; So His Highnesse hath great cause to condemne the obstinacy of all such, as in a time of such generall conformity, and against so many good examples, shall shew themselues refractorie to that His Royall pleasure, grounded vpon important reasons of Iustice and State. And therefore His Maiestie doeth eftsoones admonish them speedily to submit themselues to that His Royall Proclamation, or else to expect the seuerity of His iustice for their wilfull contempt. And this His Maiestie declares to be extended, aswell vnto such as haue repayred, or shall repayre from their ordinary dwellings in the Countrey, vnto other Cities and Townes, as vnto the Cities of London and Westminster, and aswell vnto Widdowes, as men of quality and estate, and to be continued, not only during the time of Christmasse now instant, but in that, and in all other times and seasons of this and other yeeres, vntill His Maiestie declare His pleasure otherwise. His Maiestie intending to continue this course heereafter, for the generall good of His people: Yet allowing that Liberty which alwayes hath beene in Termes, and otherwise, to repayre to London about their necessary occasions, but not to remooue their wiues and families from their ordinary habitations in the Countrey: An innouation and abuse lately crept in, and growne frequent.

And although His Maiestie is perswaded that by this way of reuiuing the laudable and ancient housekeeping of this Realme, the poore, and such as are most pinched in times of scarcity and want, will be much releeued and comforted; yet that nothing may be omitted that may tend to their succour

44

and helpe. His Highnesse in his gracious and princely care and prouidence, hath caused certaine politique & good orders, heretofore made vpon like occasion, to be reuiued & published, intituled, Orders
appointed by His Maiestie, &c. By which the Iustices of Peace in all partes of the Realme are directed
to stay all Ingrossers, Forestallers and regrators of Corne, and to direct all owners and Farmers,
hauing Corne to spare, to furnish the markets rateably and weekely, with such quantities as reason-
ably they may and ought to doe: and some one or more of them to be present in the Market, according
to the orders, and to see diuers other Articles obserued and performed, tending to the preuention
and remedy of this inconuenience. Neuerthelesse, because His Maiestie doth well know, that the
life of these his gracious, godly, and politique constitutions dependeth vpon the carefull and diligent
execution of the same: His Highnesse doth therefore by this his Proclamation straitely charge and
command, all Sheriffes, Iustices of Peace, Maiors, Bayliffes, and other his Officers and Sub-
iects whatsoeuer, That they take knowledge of the sayd Orders, and obserue, and cause the same to
bee obserued, as shall appertaine vnto them: And that they vse all possible endeauours, by execution
of the aforesaid orders, and of the good and wholsome Lawes in that behalfe, and by all other good
meanes, that the Markets may be supplied with plenty of corne, and at reasonable prizes, and the
poore set on worke and releeued, His Maiestie declaring, that (amongst other seruices which hee expe-
cteth from those persons of quality, who either before were, or vpon this, and his late Proclamation
shall reside in the Country) this before remembred is one of especiall importance: And withall, his
Maiestie hauing thus carefully prouided for releefe of his poore sort of Subiectes, doeth declare and
strictly charge and command, that if any vnder pretence of pouerty and want, shall leaue their ordinary labour, or assemble together in vnfit maner, or otherwise insolently behaue themselues, that
they be corrected and punished according to their demerits.

Giuen at Our Court at Whitehall, the two and twentieth day of December, in the twentieth yeere of Our
Reigne of England, France, and Ireland, and of Scotland the fiue and fiftieth.

God saue the King.

¶ Imprinted at London by Bonham Norton and Iohn Bill,
Printers to the Kings most Excellent Maiestie.
M. DC. XXII.

Thomas Trevelyon (b. c1548)
Pictorial commonplace book
Manuscript, 1608
Shelf mark: V.b. 232
The Gift of Lessing J. Rosenwald

Ten of the calendar illustrations from Trevelyon's
commonplace book depict agricultural or domestic
work. The captions provide information about the
image as well as basic facts about the length of the day
and night, twilight hours, and number of days in the
month. Health and dietary practices show through
the verses. Trevelyon repeats the thought that eating
uncooked fruit was dangerous (September), although
"much eaten." Blood letting was avoided in winter
months, as were baths. Hospitality for the poor is
shown in December's image.

James I
*The inquisition taken at _____ the _____ day of _____
in the_____ yeere of the raigne of James _____ before
_____deputie unto _____ esquire, clarke of the market
of his majesties. . .houshold, within the verge. . .of the
price of graine, victuals, horsemeat, lodgings, and other
things rated and taxed, in maner and forme following*
No place, 1610?
Broadsheet
Shelf mark: STC 8455

James I
*A proclamation for reformation of the great abuses in
weights and measures, and for the due execution of the
Office of Clerke of the market*
London, 1619
Sheet 4 of 4 broadsheets
Shelf mark: STC 8592

James I
*By the King. A proclamation for reliefe of the poore,
and remedying the high price of corne*
London, 1622
2 broadsheets
Shelf mark: STC 8698
(illustrated at far left and left)

then sett them on the fire, then boyle them
apace, that the liquor may rise, skiming them
very purely, and looke to them very well, for
the colour will soon bee gone, and they will
ber quickely boyled.

To make cleare Cakes of Gooseberries.

Take your Gooseberries, and pick them, and put
them into a Gally pot, and stop it close, and then
set it in a Skillet of water (but let the water
boyle before you put in your pot) and when it
hath stood about a quarter of an hour, or more,
you may try if any of the cleare will poure
from them, through a Strainer, but you must
doe it very carefully, not brusing the Gooseberries
at all for feare it will bee thicke, and you
must keepe your jeuce warme till you use it,
then take dubble refine sugar, finely beaten,
and wett it, and boyle it, then put in your jeuce
and sett it on the fire, when it is ready to boyle
(but it must not boyle) then put it into Sacers,
and soe dry it as you doe white marmelets;
you must take a pound and an halfe of sugar
to a pound of jeuce, and if it bee a hot sun-
shine day you may set it in the Sun, and
when you thinke they bee dry enough, you
may cut them off what fashion you please.

APPENDIX I: MRS. SARAH LONGE HER RECEIPT BOOKE, C1610

Introduction by Heidi Brayman Hackel, Oregon State University
Transcription by Rachel Doggett and E. Dever Powell

INTRODUCTION

Mistress Sarah Longe is one of the many early modern women who emerge from the historical record because of a single striking document. Her recipe book, which is transcribed below, provides a glimpse of her domestic world, as it reveals both her proficiencies and her resources for running a household. This small book hints at the range of responsibilities typical of early seventeenth-century housewives, and it testifies to one of the roles of literacy in the lives of non-aristocratic women.

Sarah Longe's use of the title "Mistress" instead of "Lady" places her as one of the respectable middling sort, the wife perhaps of a successful tradesman or a member of the lesser gentry. While she seems not to have been a noblewoman, she had enough contact with members of the aristocracy to include in her book a remedy "approved of by La[dy] Parsons" and a recipe for biscuits that "King James, and his Queene have eaten with much liking." And, like her use of the honorific "Mistress" to describe herself, the inclusion of gold leaf as an ingredient in one recipe suggests that she oversaw a household of some means. As the mistress of such a household, Sarah Longe would have been responsible for bearing and raising her children, caring for the sick, supervising her servants, perhaps educating the female servants, and producing or overseeing the production of food and clothing for the household. (Mendelson and Crawford, 303–313) Her *Receipt Booke*, therefore, would have served as both a guide to and a record of her management of the garden, kitchen, and distillery.

In the index at the back of the volume, Longe divides her recipes into three categories: "Preserves & Conserves," "Cokery," and "Phisike & Chirurgery." Discrete in the index, the culinary and medicinal recipes are intermingled in the volume itself. Surprising though it may be to us, this juxtaposition of recipe and remedy appears throughout the period in printed household guides and in other women's manuscript volumes.[1] Gervase Markham's popular guide, *The English Huswife* (1615), for example, combines household recipes and medicinal remedies under the rubric of "all the worthy knowledges which doe belong to [the housewife's] vocation." (R2v) While less skilled than the professional "Practitioner," Markham's exemplary housewife should be prepared to cure "those ordinary sicknesses which daily perturbe" the members of her household. (R2v-R3r) Longe's contemporary, Lady Margaret Hoby, chronicled in her diary many instances of tending to the sick, preparing purgatives, dressing wounds, even performing exploratory surgery.[2] While Longe does not demonstrate in her book quite the proficiency in "Phisike & Chirurgery" that Hoby does in her diary, she nevertheless records a range of cures for headaches, coughs, and flatulence, all of which clearly fell under the housewife's domain. These remedies are the most fully indexed—and so perhaps the most consulted—entries in her book.

Among the many skills displayed in Sarah Longe's *Receipt Booke* is her literacy, her ability, that is, to write and use this book of household management. Literacy rates for early modern England have proven notoriously difficult to determine: contemporary accounts provide conflicting estimations of the population's literacy, and historians' quantitative studies obscure the variety of partial literacies common in the period.[3] The most comprehensive study available, which is based on the presence of signatures or marks on legal documents, attributes to women "massive illiteracy" because very few women signed their names on legal documents in the sixteenth and

To make Cherrie Marmelet.

Take 5 pound of Cherries, you must weigh them
with their stones in them, after stone
them, then take one pound of sugar such as
you make marmelet with, and put your
Cherries and your sugar both together into
the pan, or skillet which you will make it
in; but beate your sugar very well: and soe
lett it boyle as you doe other marmelett, and
when you thinke it is boyled enough, put it
into your Boxes or glasses as fast as you can.

To make sugar Cakes.

Take a pound of butter, and wash it in rose-water,
and halfe a pound of sugar, and halfe a douzen
spoonefulls of thicke Creame, and the yolkes
of 4 Eggs, and a little mace finely beaten,
and as much fine flower as it will wett, and
worke it well together, then roll them out
very thin, and cut them with a glasse, and
pricke them very thicke with a great pin,
and lay them on plates, and soe bake them
gently.

To make another Bisket.

Take halfe a pound of sugar, as much flower,
11 Eggs, leave out all the whites but two,
with 2 or 3 spoonefulls of water, beate it 2
hours, and then put in a few anniseeds, and
a few Carroway seeds, bake it an hour, then

× rose-water.

seventeenth centuries. (Cressy, 128, 145) For the first decade of the 1600s, when Sarah Longe probably wrote her recipe book, female signature illiteracy was 91% in London and 94% in Norfolk and Suffolk. (Cressy, 144) However, signature literacy rates greatly underestimate the number of people who could read. (Thomas, 103; Spufford, 22) For, in early modern England, the skills of reading and writing were taught separately; many people, accordingly, must have been able to read but not write. (Spufford, 19–44) Other members of Sarah Longe's household, therefore, may have been able to use her book of recipes, even if they could not write themselves. Women, especially, are likely to have been partially literate since schools often excluded writing, but not reading, from the curriculum for girls. (Spufford, 34–36; Sanders, 169–170) In her ability to both read and write, Longe was perhaps unusual in the female population at large; she may have owed her literacy to the benefits of her class, to the enthusiasm of a parent, or to her own curiosity and diligence. The appearance of the *Receipt Booke* further suggests that Longe owned other books: the generous margins and the absence of other marks in the book may persuade us that Longe had access to other paper on which to scribble accounts, practice her penmanship, or record significant dates.

Sarah Longe's *Receipt Booke* belongs to a category of domestic writings that, like women's diaries, letters, and other household manuals, reveal not only women's roles within the household but also their participation in larger communities. Whether Sarah Longe copied recipes from other women's books or transcribed them from conversations, her literacy connected her kitchen and her distillery to those of Lady Parsons, Mr. Aires, and Mr. Triplett, even as her biscuits linked her table to the King and Queen's.

1   Suzanne Hull provides an overview of contemporary printed household guides (37–45); two early seventeenth-century manuscript recipe books are accessible in modern editions by Hess and Spurling. For discussions of women's household duties in the kitchen and the sickroom, see Spurling, 17–20, and Mendelson and Crawford, 303–313.

2   See, for example, her diary entries of 12 July 1600, 28 April 1601, and 26 August 1601.

3   Bennett discusses contemporary assessments of literacy early in the period (27–29); Kiefer offers a succinct overview of the issue in his appendix, "Elizabethan Literacy" (268–274).

Note: The following is a literal transcription of the manuscript. Punctuation that has been added for clarity and a few changes to spelling appear within square brackets. When abbreviations have been expanded, the added letter is underlined. A few words that were unclear are followed by question marks within parentheses.

. . . .

1   **To make Snow.**

Take a pint of thicke sweete Creame,
and halfe a pint of Sack, and halfe a
pound of Sugar, and the white of two Eggs
well beaten, and a pretty deale of Limon,
and mingle all this together, and put it into
a pretty big earthen Pan, or Bason, and
take a pretty big birchen rod, and beate it
till the froth doth rise, and then take it
of[f] with a stirre, and put it into the thing
you would have it goe in, (it should bee
a glasse Sillibubbe pot, if you have it[;] if not,
a white creame dish will serve[;] you should
lett it stand a pretty while before you eate
it, because it should settle with a little
kinde of drinke at the bottome, like a
Sillibubbe.

To make a Goosebery Foole.

Take two handfulls of greene Gooseberies, and
pricke them, then scald them very soft, and
poure the water from them very cleane, and
breake them very small, and season them
with rose-water, and sugar, and then take
a quart of Creame, or butter, and put in a little
mace, and sett it on the fire, (letting it boyle)
and then take it of[f], and take out the Mace,
and poure it into the Gooseberies, and stirre it
about, and lett it stand till it bee cold, and then
eate it.

. . . .

To make Conserve of Roses.   2

Take rose-buds, clip of[f] the white at the bottome[;]
then weigh them, and take to a pound of roses

3 pound of lofe sugar[;] beate the sugar very
fine[;] beate the roses in a stone morter[;] strane
in the sugar in the beating of them[;] beate them
one hour or longer, till they are very finely
beaten[;] then put it up in your Gally pot.

To make a White-pot.

Take a quart of Creame, a lofe of bread,
and slice it thin (the crust being taken from
it)[,] one Nutmegge, and stirre it, a pound of Currence, and sett it on the fire a quarter of an
hour, and boyle it thicke, (keeping it stirr'd)[,]
and take 7 Eggs, and beate them, and take
3 whites from them, and take a quarter
of a pound of sugar, put the Eggs, and sugar
into the rest, and boyle it, then put it in a
dish, and bake it in an Oven for the space of
an hour; you may put the marrow of 2 bones
into it when you put it into the Oven, and
for want of that, you may put in a little
slice of butter.

To preserve Gooseberies.

Stone your Goose-beries, and lay them in faire
water an hour, and shift the water once or

. . . .

3

twice, and prick them round with a great
pin[;] then take a pound and an halfe of sugar,
and a wine-pint of water; melt your sugar,
and boyle your sirrope, and skim it well[;] then
put in your Gooseberies, and lett them stand,
and boyle an hour or two[;] then take them
of[f], and sett them by, 2 or 3 days in a glasse,
(but doe not cover them till they be cold)[;]
then boyle them upon a quick fire, till
the sirrope gelly, but not so high, for feare
they turne red.

To preserve Cherries.

Cut of[f] the stalks, and then weigh them,
stems and all; To a pound of Cherries put
3 quarters of a pound of sugar; put your
sugar into a pan, and poure 5 sponefulls
of water into it[;] then sett it on the fire, and
boyle it, and skim it, and then put in your
Cherries; boyle them on a quicke fire
(taking them of[f] now and then, stirring
them about the pan) and when the sirrope
will gelly they are enough; you must stone
the Cherries after they bee weighed;
when your Cherries bee boyl'd, poure them
out into a silver dish, and lett them
stand till they bee cold[;] then poure them
into a glass; you may put to a pound of or-
dinarie Cherries about 3 quarters of a pound of
sugar.

· ·

To make red marmelett   4

Take Quinces and pare them, quarter them,
and core them[;] then take a pound of them,
and a pound of sugar, and halfe a pint of
water, and put all in a Skillet, and when it
is hot, take a good many of the cores of the
Quinces and tye them up in a peece of lawne,
and put them in[;] then cover them, and lett
them boyle softly for 2 hours[;] then take out
the Cores, and wring them betweene 2 trenchers,
and then breake the Quinces, and cover them,
and lett them boyle apace, and stirre them
till they bee enough, and soe put it into boxes.

To make white Marmelet

Take Quinces and par-boyle them very tender,
then pare them, and scrape the pap from
the Core[;] then take a pound of the pap and
dry it in a dish a little while, and take a
pound of sugar finely beaten, and wet your
sugar with 2 or 3 sponefulls of water[;] boyle

your sugar againe, and then put in your
pap that is a drying, and stirre it well together, and sett it on the fire till it bee made
to boyle[;] then take it of[f], and put it into
glasses, and sett it in a stove till it bee
canded.

· ·

5   **To make rice-puddings**

Take a pound of Rice, boyle it in a pottle of
milke till it bee thicke as you may cutt it
with a knife when it is cold, and take halfe
a pound of Almonds, and grind them very
small in a stone morter (adding now and
then in the grinding a sponefull of milke
that hath bin boyled and cold againe)[;]
put in 3 pound of Beefe Seuett, 2 penny
loves grated, one ounce of Mace, 3 Nut-
megg's, the yelkes of 15 Eggs, one pound
of sugar, a little rose-water, and fine salt[;]
Temper all these with Creame, being
boyl'd, and cold againe, and lett it not bee
tempered too thin.

To make a Cake

Take halfe a bushell of fflower, 8 pound of Currence, and 5 pound of butter, and boyle it
by it selfe, and skim it, 3 pints of Creame, and
boyle it, 3 quarters of a pound of sugar, one
Ounce of mace, one Ounce of Nut-megg's,
halfe an Ounce of Cinamon, a little Ginger,
halfe a quarter of a pint of Rose-water, 10
Eggs, (halfe the whites) and halfe a pound of
Carroway-comfetts, one quart of yeest, and
lett it stand in the Oven an hour and an
halfe.
Note:
make 3 holes in the
flower, and put the
Eggs in one hole,
the melted butter
in the other, and

the yeest in the 3d.,
and have a care that
you scald not the ye[e]st
w.th the Creame when
you mingle the Cake.

. . . .

To make Snow-Creame. 6

Take a quart of Creame, and put in a little
large mace, and then sett it on the fire,
and lett it boyle, and then take it of[f], and
poure it into a bason, and take the mace
and lett it stand till it bee almost cold,
and then poure it into a platter, and
put in a sponefull of good Runnett, and
then stirr it together, soe lett it stand till
it bee cold.

To make a Posset without milke.

Take 12 or 14 Eggs, beate them very well with
halfe a pound of sugar, saving from it soe much
sugar as to straw on it when it is made, and
with halfe a white-lofe grated stirre it well-
together[;] then take a pint of aile, and halfe
a pint of Sack, a few cloves and mace, and
halfe a nut-megge[;] breake it in 2. or 3. peeces,
and put in the spice into the Sack and aile
together in a Skillett on the fire, and as soone
as it seetheth, put in the Eggs (the Skillett
being still on the fire) and keeping it very
well stirr'd till you perceive that it is as
thicke as you will have it[;] then presently
power it out into your bason, and if you
thinke it too cleare, sett the bason on the

. . . .

7
Colles a little while, but stirre it aboute[;]
then straw on the rest of the sugar with
beaten Cinamon.

How to dry Cherries.

Take your Cherries and stone them, and to 5^{li'} of
Cherries take one pound of sugar, and halfe a
pint of water[;] you may take pouder sugar,
but if it bee cource you must clarify it, then
put in your Cherries, and boyle them a quarter
of an hour apace[;] then take them of[f] the
fire, and lett them stand till they bee cold[;]
then take them out, and lay them upon
plates with their holes downewards, and
flatt them with your finger[;] then sett them
into a warme Oven, or in the Sun, and dry
them, but an Oven is the best; when they
are a little dry you must shift them on
cleane plates, and when they are enough,
you must tye them up close in paper, and
soe they will keepe all the yeare.

To preserve Barberies.

Take a pound and an halfe of sugar, and melt
it with halfe a pint of water, and skim it
very cleane[;] then take a pound of barberies
ready stoned and put them into the liquor,
and soe sett them till they bee throughly warme[;]

. . . .

8
Then sett them on the fire[;] then boyle them
apace, that the liquor may rise, skiming them
very purely, and looke to them very well, for
the colour will soone bee gone, and they will
bee quickely boyled.

To make cleare Cakes of Gooseberies.

Take your Gooseberries, and pick them, and put
them into a Gally pot, and stop it close, and then
set it in a Skillett of water (but lett the water
boyle before you put in your pot) and when it
hath stood about a quarter of an hour, or more,

you may try if any of the cleare will poure
from them, through a Strainer, but you must
doe it very carefully, not brusing the Gooseberies
at all for feare it will bee thicke, and you
must keepe your jeuice warme till you use it;
then take dubble refine sugar, finely beaten,
and wett it, and boyle it[;] then put in your jeuce
and sett it on the fire[;] when it is ready to boyle
(but it must not boyle) then put it into sacers
and soe dry it as you doe white marmelet[;]
you must take a pound and an halfe of sugar
to a pound of jeuce, and if it bee a hot sun
shine day you may set it in the Sun, and
when you thinke they bee dry enough, you
may cut them off what fashion you please.

. . . .

9   To make Cherrie Marmelet.

Take 5 pound of Cherries[;] you must weigh them
with their stones in them[;] after stone
them[;] then take one pound of sugar such as
you make marmelet with, and put your
Cherries and your sugar both together into
the pan, or skillet which you will make it
in, but beate your sugar very well: and soe
lett it boyle as you doe other marmelett, and
when you thinke it is boyled enough, put it
into your Boxes or glasses as fast as you can.

To make sugar Cakes.

Take a pound of butter, and wash it in rose-water,
and halfe a pound of sugar, and halfe a douzen
sponefulls of thicke Creame, and the yelkes
of 4 Eggs, and a little mace finely beaten,
and as much fine flower as it will wett, and
worke it well together[;] then roll them out
very thin, and cut them with a glasse, and
pricke them very thicke with a great pin,
and lay them on plates, and soe bake them
gently.

To make another Bisket.

Take halfe a pound of sugar, as much flower,
11 Eggs, leave out all the whites but two,
with 2 or 3 sponefulls of rosewater[;] beate it 2
hours, and then put in a few anniseeds, and
a few Carroway seeds[;] bake it an hour, then

. . . .

10

take it forth, and shift it[;] then you must
dry it againe in the Sun or Oven.

To make Metheglen.

Take of the best Condit-water, and the best
and purest hony you can gett[;] put them
together in a tub, and beate them together
till it bee strong enough to beare a new
lade Egg from the bottome[;] then sett it over
the fire, and put into it a little rose-mary,
Time, marjorum, and winter savery ty'd
up in a bundle, (if you please you may
put in Maiden-haire, Liver-wort, or
any other herbs, as you thinke fitt)[;] then
make a little fine bagg of Linnen, and
put into it 3. or 4. races of ginger, 2. or 3. Nutmeggs, a little Cloves, and mace, and if
you will a little Cinamon[;] sew it up, and
put it into the boyling[;] lett it boyle one
whole hour, skiming it all the while[;] then
poure it out into Earthen pans, and soe lett
it stand till next morning[;] then poure
all the cleare of the pans into a good
vessell, one that hath binn used with
sacke or white-wine, and hang your
bag of spices in it[;] soe stop it close, and
lett it stand at least 2 moneths before
you drinke of it[;] then draw it into bottles
if you please[;] it will be beater; you may make

. . . .

it with a lemon pill put into the vessell;
if you intend to keepe it, make it the
stronger of hony, and spice, if to drinke
at 2 moneths End, lett the Egg only rise
from the bottome without swiming.

**A speciall water for sore Eyes if a man
have lost his Sight 5 yeares[;] if it be
possible it will restore it within 40 days.**

Take small dye Rue, fennel, verven, Egrimony,
Bitany Scabius, hounes stongue, Eye bright, pim-
pernet sage[;] distill all these together, with a
little urin of a man-child, and 5 graines of
ffrankinsence[;] drop of ye same every night
into the sore Eyes.

For sore nipples.

Take house-leeke, marigold leaves, plantine
Ribwort, Ledwell parsley, Beesewax, of each
a like quantity[;] boyle y^m in fresh butter
unwashed, while it is enough[;] then stirre it,
and keepe it for your use.

To preserve Barberies.

Take a pound and halfe of sugar, and melt it
with halfe a pint of water, and skim it
very cleane[;] then take a pound of Bar-

. . . .

beries ready stoned, and put them into the
liquor, and then lett 'um lye till they be through
warme[;] then sett them on the fire, and
lett them boyle a little while gently, taking
them of[f] againe a while[;] then againe
boyle them a pace that the liquor may
rise, scuming them very cleane, and

looke to them very well, for they will be
quickly be boyled, and the Colour will soone
be gone.

To preserve Apricockes, and dry them.

ffirst gather your Apricockes before they are
ripe[;] then a day after they be gathered
stone them, and paire them very thin,
and to a pound of apricocks put a pound of
sugar, and lett your Apricocks lye in the
sugar covered for 2 hours untill the sugar
be moist as it will melt without water[;]
Then put your Sugar, and apricockes upon
a soft fire, that they boyle not in halfe
an hour[;] then let them boyle very softly
for halfe an hour, or more, turning y^m
often that they breake not[;] when you
thinke they be enough put them into a
deepe glasse, and the Sirrope into a
Silver dish, and lett the Sirrope

. . . .

seeth a little[;] then poure into your apricocks
the same, and soe let it stand uncovered
untill the next day[;] then cover them,
and when they have laine a weeke in
the Sirrope, take them out, and lay y^m
on a faire glass, and put them into a stove,
or some cleane place, where they may have
some aire of the fire, and every day
turne them uppon cleane glasses untill
they be through dry.

**A more approved way to preserve
Apricockes.**

Take ripe Apricockes, and sun them, and
paire them[;] Then take a pound of lofe
sugar finely beaten, and put it into a pan,
and melt it with halfe a pint of water,

and boyle it up that it be throughly melted
to skum[;] then take your pound of apricockes that are paired[;] then put them into
the liquor, and there let them stand a
quarter of an hour, till they be throughly
warme; then sett them on the fire for y^e
space of halfe an hour, taking them of[f]
one 2. or 3. times in the space of halfe
an hour[;] then take them of[f] from the
fire, boyling them gently, covering y^m

. . . .

with a cloath and a dish, and soe lett them
stand till they are cold[;] then sett them
on the fire, boyling them gently till you
thinke they are halfe boyled[;] then take
them of[f], and let them stand till next
day, and then boyle them up, but put
them not into your glasses untill they be
cold.

Note: If you please you may make your water
that you melt your sugar withall to be
halfe of pippins.

To sun the Apricockes.

Boyle greene pippins in water, and
when your liquor is strong of the pippins
then straine it out, and use the liquor
instead of water for preserving the
Apricockes.

To preserve Damsons.

You must preserve damsons eaven as you
doe Apricockes, but take a pound and
quarter of sugar, to a pound of damsons,
and take noe other liquor but halfe a
pint of water.

. . . .

15 To preserve greene Apricockes.

ffirst gather your Apricockes before they have
any stone in them with the stalkes on, and
waigh them[;] and take to a pound of Apricockes a pound of sugar[;] then take a skillet
of faire water and make it boyle, and put in
your Apricockes, and make them boyle
till they have lost their Colour[;] then take
them out of that water and put them into
another Skillet of water that boyleth, and
let them boyle till they be tender, and
take them out of the water againe, and put
them againe into the other water, and sett
them on a few Embers, and lett them simper
till they come to their Colour againe[;] and
then take them up, and beate your sugar
very fine, and put it in your preserving
pan, and lay in your Apricockes, and
take a little of the liquor and drop upon
them all, and soe preserve them.

To preserve Quinces Red.

Take a pound of Quinces ready pared, and
Cored, a pound and halfe of lofe sugar, a
wine pint of water, and make your
liquor, and keepe a quarter of a pound
of sugar out to strain upon them

. . . .

as they boyle to keep them from breaking
and when your liquor hath boyled, and is
skumed, then put in your Quinces, and
boyle them gently at first, and cover
them till they be red, and then boyle
them up faster till they be enough.

To preserve Quinces white.

Take 8 pound of pouder sugar, and a pint and
halfe of water, with the whites of 2 Eggs[;]
stirre these well together in your preserving pan[;] then set it over the fire,
and lett it boyle 4 or 5 warmes (you must
not stirre it while it is upon the fire)[;]
when it hath boyled you must straine it
into a cleane pan, and sett the sirrope
upon the fire till it be boyled.
Take 3 pound of Quinces[,] boyle them in
faire water till they be tender[;] you
must lett the water boyle before you
put in the Quinces, and when they
are tender boyled you must paire them,
and core them[;] then put your Quinces
into the Sirrope that you have made
and when they have boyled a pretty
while, you must take halfe a pound of
lofe sugar finely beaten, and put all

. . . .

17
the halfe pound in the boyling[;] boyle it
till you find the sirrope thicke; you must
preserve them upon a quick fire, and put
a little musk in them when you have
found them enough; Then put them up
into your glasses or potts: before you take
up your Quinces, take up some of the
Sirrope into a little dish, and when
they are both cold enough, then put
the sirrope to cover the Quinces.

To preserve Wallnutts.

Take your Walnutts when they be greene,
and pare all the greene of[f] them; then
prick 3 pricks in every walnut[;] then
scald them as you doe other things[;] when
they be scalded take them forth, and
lett them lye in water 2 or 3 day's[;]

and shift the water twice a day[;] then
take them forth[;] then take the 6th
part of a Clove and stick it in one end of
each wallnut[;] soe put them in sugar,
and preserve them as other fruite.

. . . .

To preserve Wallnutts the Physical way.   18

Take a pound of walnuts, and a pound of sugar,
and halfe a pint, or a pint of Damask
rose-water[;] scald the walnuts, and shift
them twice[;] then put them to the rose-
water and sugar, and stew them as you
doe pruines, and soe keepe them all the
yeare for your use.

To make sirrope of Roses.

Take Damask roses, and pick them, and
put them into a bottle of water as many
as you can well thrust in, and keepe it
in a close pott in a warme place, and
shift it every second day till it bee 9.
times shifted[;] then straine it, and
put to a quart of liquor one pound and
halfe of sugar[;] you must shift them
from the seeds.

How to Clarifie sugar.

Take the whites of 2 Eggs, and beate them
with a little birchen rod very well[;]
then put halfe into your sugar that
you melt with your water[;] then when
it boyles up put the other halfe in,

. . . .

and soe lett it boyle 2. or 3. warmes[;] then
straine it into a dish; then wash your
pann very cleane, and put in your
clarify'd liquor[;] then put in your
plumbes, and soe preserve them.

To make Biskets of Almons
very dainty, and knowne
of few.

Take a pound of Almons, blanch them,
then beate them in a morter[;] then
put in a little rose-water to them,
that they may not turne to an Oyle
in their beating; when they are
beaten very small take them up, and
put them into a Dish[;] then take
halfe a pound of sugar beaten very
small, and put to them the whites
of 4. Eggs, with a little Quantity of
musk, and Ambergrease[;] then
beate it altogether a quarter of an
hour, then put it upon papers in
what fashion you will. You must
be carefull in the making of it,
that it be not coloured to[o] much.

. . . .

Another Bisket.   20

Take 3 quarters of a pound of sugar,
beate it fine, as much flower, take
a little handfull of Anniseeds, and as
much Coriander seeds[;] beate them,
and search them fine[;] take 7. Eggs
and leave out 2 of the whites[;] put in
2 sponefulls of rose-water, mingle
them together, and beate it an hour
and halfe[;] when you put it into y^e
oven, cast fine sugar over the top
of it.

To make another Bisket, whereof
King James, and his Queene
have eaten with much liking.

Take a pound and quarter of sugar, and a
pound of fflower very finely boulted, and
after finely searched, you must beate the
sugar very fine, and then search it through
a fine lawne search, and mingle the
flower and sugar together[;] then take
12 Eggs whereof you must take but halfe
the whites[;] first beate the Eggs with 3. or 4.
Sponefulls of rose-water[;] then put the
flower and sugar that are mingled to-

. . . .

gether to the Eggs[;] then beate them one hour
together[;] a little before you put them into
your Oven, put a few Caroway seeds, and
Aniseeeds into it, and cutt your plates before
you put on the stuff, and the oven must
be noe hotter then for a Tart.

To stop the bleeding of a wound.

Take a peece of an Old hatt, and burne
it in the fire to a Cole[;] then grind it to
powder, and straw it into the wound.

A remedy for such as are subject to miscarry.

Take a quart or 2 of stronge Aile, and a
pound of Currence, an ounce of Nutmegg's,
and prick them full of holes, and take pith
of 2 oxen, and one handfull of Nipp, &
an handfull of Pimpernell, one handfull of Clary, and boyle them together,
till a pint be boyled away[;] brush the
Currence, and the Pith of the Oxen,
and put them in againe, and boyle it
againe, and then drinke it morning, and
Evening warmed.

Another for the same Remidy.

22

Take a little Clary, a little Comfery, a little
knott grass, the Pith of an Ox[;] boyle these
in a quart of Aile, till halfe be wasted[;]
then straine it, and take every Morning a
Poringer full of it, and thicken it with
an Egg, and put in it some Cinamon, &
Sugar.

To make Conserve of Barberies

Boyle your Barberies in an Earthen pott,
in a kittle of water while they be tender[;]
then straine them through a cloath[;] then
take a pound of sugar, and wett it with 4.
or 5. sponefulls of water[;] then boyle it to
sugar againe, (continually stirring it)[;]
then put in a pound of your Barberies,
that you have strained into your sugar,
stirring it[;] then set it on the fire, and
let it boyle halfe a douzen warmes, -
then take it of[f] from the fire, and scum
it[;] then put it into your glasses, and
set it in a stove, and soe candy it.

23 A receipt for my Capp.

Take Bittony, red sage, red-rose leaves,
sweet Margerum, Cowslip flowers,
and penyriall, of either an equall Quantity[;] lett them be all well dried, and
beaten into a gross pouder, and put to
it Nutmeggs, Cloves, and mace all pounded,
a little quantity to a good handfull of each
of the herbes[;] take halfe an ounce of each
of these spices[;] lett all be mingled together[;] take some of the pouder, and
quilt it with some Bumbast, in a Capp
of a fitt bignes for your head.

A receipt for a Cordiall for a woman that is in danger to Miscarry.

Take the yelkes of halfe a dousen new laid
Eggs, and halfe a pint of plantine water, and halfe a pint of red-wine, and
season it with Cinamon, and sugar, and soe
drinke it[;] also take the Top of a wheaten
lofe, and tost it, and stick it with Cloves,
and wett it with Muscadine, and lay it
to her Navill.

For a stinking, or poysen of Snakes, or adders

Take Bittony, Egrimony, and rusty bakon,
and beate them fine together, and lay it
to the wound, and it will keepe it from
rankling[;] it is also good for the biting
of a madd dogg to keepe it from rankling, or to draw out a Thorne.

To make ffritters.

Take 3 pints of Milke, a quart of aile,
and make a Posset of these[;] stirre it all
together, and lett it stand till it be pretty
Cold[;] then put in 16 Eggs, (taking
out halfe the whites), and put in flower,
and make it as thicke as you would have
it for the ffritters[;] then put in good store
of Apples sliced thin[;] keepe the butter
warme, for it if be cold the fritters
will be heavy; fry them on a quick fire,
with store of beefe suett.

25 **To boyle a Pike.**

Take your Pike and open him, and wash him
cleane, and salt him on the Inside[;] then
boyle it in water and salt[;] lett the water
boyle a pace before you put him in[;] put
in a good bundle of sweet herbs, with some
rose-mary[;] lett it boyle altogether, till it
be boyled enough[;] take 3 sponefulls of
white-wine, one sponefull or 2 of Vinigar,
2 sponefulls of sugar, 3. or 4. yelkes of Eggs[;]
beate it altogether in a dish[;] then take
halfe a pound of sweet butter, a nutmegge
grated, and a little beaten ginger, and
worke it in your Butter very well, your
butter being cold[;] then put it into the
Eggs, and wine[;] sett it on the fire, &
stirre it till it be very Thick in a
dish[;] then take your Pike up, and
dish it, and poure this broth on it.

. . . .

To make a Hagis.   26

Take a chalves Chadarne, and parboyle it[;]
when it is cold mingle it fine, with a pound
of Beefe suet, a penny-lofe grated, some rose-
mary, time, winter-savery, and penyriall,
of all a small handfull, a little Cloves,
Mace, nutmegge, and Cinamon, one
quarter of a pound of Currence, a little
sugar, a little salt, rose-water, all these
mixt together[;] wett with 16 yolkes of
Eggs, put it in a Sheeps panch, and boyle it.

To make Plague water.

Take Cowslip flowers, Red weed, Roman
wormewood, Mugwort, Horshound, Pimpernell, Rice, Sage, Saladine, Motherwort, Worm
wood, Burnet, Iurmentall, Sorrell, Elli-
compaine-rootes, ffeatherfew, Balme,
Dragon, Angelico, Marrigolds, Rose-

mary halfe a pound, Bron(?) may weeds,
Scabius, Egrimony, Bittony, Cardis, Endiff,
Sotherne-wood, then Birchlott, Macthaline,
Sinkfall, of each a quarter of a pound,
shred them very small, and lay them a
steepe 24. hours in 3 quarts of whitewine[;]

. . . .

27
Then still them, in a limbick, or still[;]
then save the first as strongest, and
soe a 2 and 3 sort.

**An Excellent Plaster to keep
a woman from miscarring.**

Take of the choisest Mastick 4. drames, gum
Elemie halfe an Ounce, Burgandie pitch 3
drames, Benjamin, and Dragons blade, of
each 2 drames; melt all these, and straine
them, and add to them 2 drames of the
Trochises, called Alepta Muscata, one
drame of Venice Turpintine a little boyled,
3 drames of the plaster of red lead made
of Oile of Quinces, halfe an Ounce of
Bees-wax, one drame and halfe of
Indian Balsome, 2 scruples of Oile
of Spike[;] make these all into one plaster,
and spread there of upon your leather,
on[e] for the region of your back, and another for the lower Region of the belly.

Sirrope of Violetts.

Take a reasonable quantity of Violetts,
and pick them, then weigh them, and
take to a quarterne of Violetts halfe a
pound of sugar, and halfe a pint of

. . . .

water[;] then shred the violetts very small
and beate the sugar very fine[;] then
take halfe a pint of water and make
it boyle in a cleane Skillet, and put
in the sugar, and skim it very cleane[;]
then put the Violetts into a gally pott,
and put the liquor to them seething
hott, and soe stirre it about, and cover
it close, and lett it stand soe till next
morning[;] then straine it, and boyle
it up to a Sirrope, and soe keepe it.
Note: A quarter of a pint of Violetts will make
a pint of sirrope.

Hony of roses.

Take red-rose budds, and white clipt
of them[;] take a pint of the best hony,
and stirre it in as many leaves as
you can[;] then sett it in a Skillet
of water over the fire[;] there lett it
stand while it is ready to boyle[;] then
sett it in the sun, shift it 3. or 4. times
every 2 day beating of it every time.

. . . .

29 To make Chynie Broth

Take one Ounce and halfe of Chiny, infuse
it in a pottle of running water 24. hours,
then stirre it, and put in a Cock Chicken,
a handfull of reasons of the sun stoned, a
handfull of Currence, a blaid of mace,
a top of rose-mary, a quarter of an Ounce
of red Sanders, a quarter of an Ounce
of white Sanders, and thick it with the
bottome of a white-lofe[;] when it is boyled
take out the Chicken, and straine the
broth before the party must drinke
thereof, and lett him drinke it 3 hours
before dinner fasting, and a draft at

4. a Clock in the after-noone, with a
little sugar; the broth will last but
3. days good.

An approved medicine called
purging aile, to be taken
every spring, and fall

Take 4. Gallons of aile-wort, the strongest
you can gett, boyle it till comes to 3 or
there abouts[;] lett it be of the first spent
as Brewers calls it[;] soe tun it up with
store of Barme, that it may worke
well, but against you tun it up, make a

. . . .

bag, and slitt it through, or thrust
a haisle stick through it, and soe
fasten it to the sticke, that it comes
not within 3 Inches of the barrells
bottome, nor flote at the topp; with
the barme then put these things
following into the bagg:

2 Ounces of Bay-berries huld
2 Ounces of Anniseeds
3 Ounces of Ashen-keys brused
2 Ounces of Sasafras wood
2 Ounces of Saldeneta
2 drams of Ruburb.

Lett all these be brused to pouder, except
the Cena which must be whole, and when
the Aile leaves working, stop it up
close, leaving good store of barme
on the Top, and after 3. or 4. day's
drinke thereof halfe a pint every
morning, and in the Evening a
little lesse, but if you take a
little warme broth 2. or 3. hours after
it, it will worke the better.

. . . .

31 A purge for a man

Rubrick 3 drames, Seny 3 drames,
a little sweet fennell seed, a blade
of mace, white wine 4 sponefulls,
as much Endiffe water as will cover
it[;] infuse all these 12 hours; then
straine it, and put to it 4. sponefulls of sirrope of Roses.

The Golden Oyle.

Violetts, Primrose, Cowslips, The leaves, or
flowers of them, Sage, Margerom, Rosemary
Nip, Lavendar, rose-leaves, Smallage,
Southerne-wood, Rew, Time, Damask, ffeatherfew, Clary, Tansy, Loveage, Mint,
Camamell, Oke of Gerusalem, Peneriall,
Safforne, Hysope, Balme, White mint,
Marygold leaves, Dasy-leaves, Bay-leaves,
Dill, Piony leaves, of each of these a handfull brused in a morter[;] infuse them in a
pipkin, with a pottle of Sallet oile, and
a quart of White-wine, and lett it boyle
softly till the wine be boyled away[;]
after it is cold straine it through a
linnin-Clouth, and put it into a glass.

. . . .

32

Because all these herbes are not to
be had altogether, you must make use
of such till you can gett the rest[;] stamp
them as aforesaid, and infuse them in
the Oyle, straining them everyday,
to keep them from moulding, till the
Oile be made Compleate; This Oyle
is especially good for the Goute, or any
humour that runs up and downe in
the Ioynts[;] it is good to anoint the
stomake for any windy, or belching
Cause[;] it is good to anoint the gutts in

Cause of the Collick, and also the
raines (mixing it with the Oile of
lillies), and a good meanes to bring
downe the Stone.

A receipt for one that cannot make Water.

Let him use to Eate Aglentine Berries,
and they will force him to make water[,]
often times in a short space[;] you may keepe
them all the yeare; they will be good in
winter if you need them.

. . . .

33 ffor the Mother.

Take a dram of Methridate, dissolve it
in one Ounce and an halfe of Wormwood water[;]
drinke it 4. hours before you goe to bed.

To stint bleeding at the Nose.

Take yarrow and put into the Nostrills
of him that bleedeth[;] it will stint it
presently.

To boyle a Capon.

Take a Capon and Two Marrowbones, the
Marrow being taken out, and sett on the
fire, the Capons and the bones in a broad
mouth pott, or Kettle, and lett it seeth
till the broth be strong of the meate[;]
then take a pint of the broth, and a
pint of Renish wine, or halfe a pint of
sack, or halfe a pint of Muscadine[,]
and put into it large mace, and Cinamon
sticks, 3. or 4. Cornes of whole pepper, 3.
or 4. dates cut in the middle, and the
stones taken out[;] lett this with halfe
a quarter of sugar be boyled on a soft

fire, till halfe be consumed, then

. . . .

beate 4 or 5 Eggs throughly, and straine
them in a porrenger, with 2. or 3. sponefulls of cold Renish-wine, or verjuice[;]
then put a quarterne of sugar to the Eggs,
and still stirre it, till the sugar be melted[;]
then take the other broath from of[f] the
fire seathing, and pour out some of it
into a pottinger, and coole it[;] then
pour it all into a pipkin of broth, (One
stirring it) and soe lett it boyle one warme
with your Marrow[.] Then lay the Capon
in a Dish, and poure the broth into
it; when the Capon is almost boyled,
take it, and lay it in a platter, with
the breast upward, and scatter some
salt thereon, untill your broth be
ready[;] then boyle it a little more, and
that will make it looke white.

. . . .

35 **The Cocke water for a Consumption.**

Take a runing Cocke pull him alive, then
kill him, and when he is almost Cold,
knock him in the backe, and take out the
Intralls, and wipe him cleane, and then
put him in such a still, as you still rose-
water with, with a pottle of sack, a pottle
of new milke of a red Cow, a pound of Cur-
rance, a pound of raisons of the sun stoned,
a quarter of a pound of Dates, stoned and
Cutt small, 2 handfulls of pimpernell,
2 handfulls of Rose-mary blossoms, a
handfull of wild time, 2 handfulls of
Pineriall, 2 handfulls of Bugles
blossomes, 2 handfulls of Burgage
blossomes, an handfull of fennell rootes,
and an handfull of parsly rootes scraped,
the pitch taken out, an handfull of En-

dive leaves, an handfull of Succory leaves,
a handfull of maiden haire, a handfull
of figgs, 3 ounces of anniseeds brused, 7.
ounces of liquoras scraped, and brused[;]
still all these together with a soft fire,
putting into the glass which The water
dropeth into halfe a pound of sugar
Candy beaten small, a booke of leafe gold
cut small among the sugar, 4 graines of

. . . .

Amber-greace, 12 graines prepared pearles,
and soe lett the water drop in upon these
things in the glass[;] mingle the first water and the last both together, and
take 4. sponefulls in the morning fasting, and 4. sponefulls an hour before
supper, and shake it about the glass
before you take the water to drinke.

For a Vomitt.

Take Crocus, Merhelosuse(?), and put a
drame into a pint of sacke, and soe
keepe, and the night before you give
it shake the glass, and soe give six-
sponefulls of the wine to one that is old,
and 3. to a Child, or by weight an Ounce,
and to a Child halfe an Ounce.

Another way to make snow.

Take a pint of creame, and a little rose-
water, and the white of 2 Eggs, and as
much sugar as will sweeten it, and soe
wipe it, and take of the froath, but not
into the thing as you wold have it, and
soe lett it stand neere halfe an houre,
till it be settled to the bottome[;] then
take it out slightly into the thinge
you would have it goe in, and lay it in heapes.

37. For the Megrim, or swiming in the head

Twenty ground Ivy leaves, and one primrose roote, cleane washed, and scraped[;]
stamp them together small, with a sponefull of womans milke, (If the medicine
be for a man, it must be the milke which
a Girle suck's on, if for a woman it
must be the milke which a boy sucks)[;]
straine out the Iuice, and of that
substance take out one drop in a spone,
and sett a quill upon it, and holding
one nostrill with your finger snuffe
it up with the other, and after 3
dayes doe the like to the other nostrill,
and then noe more for a weeke.

For Expulsion of wind.

White pepper, Black pepper, of each a
peny-worth, Time, ginger, anniseeds[,]
of each a spone-full, searched, and made
into fine powder, and a penyworth
of long pepper[;] the white must be
beaten grossly. Then take a pint and
an halfe of Isopp water, and put into
it 3 quarters of a pound of sugar,

. . . .

38.

boyle it till it comes to a sirrope[;] after
Cooling, then put in your pouders, stirring
it well together, and soe keepe it in a
gally-pot if you please a yeare together.

A pouder for a weake back which never failes, approved of by La. Parsons.

Take the kernells of Acrons, white
archangle flowers, or for want of
them Pomegranette blossomes, red
Corall, and amber, of each halfe an
Ounce, Sugar candy, an Ounce, powder
them all very fine, and drinke as
much of it morning, and Evening in
beere as will lye upon sixpence[;] if
the flux be very great, then drinke
it with this distilled water.

Take Muskadine 3 pints, the inward
pith of the backe of a young bullock,
a quart of creame, a quarter of a
pound of Dates, 2 ounces of mastick,
brused Plantaine, and Knott grass, of
each 2 good handfulls[;] steepe all these
together in a bason, covered a day &
a night[;] then put it into a glasse,

. . . .

39.

still and distill it in hott water[;] this water
with this pouder will stop the flux of
the whites, eaven the runing of the
raines, and restore any weake back.

To stay the whites, and runing of the Raines. Master Aires

Take a quart of water, put into it one
Ounce of Anniseeds, and boyle it to a
pint, then straine it, and devide the
liquor into 3 parts, and put into it one
sponefull of the Iuice of red mint,
and soe drinke a mornings cold, and
nights warme for a weake or longer if
you please[;] you must make the
Iuice of mint fresh every day, &
if you put a sponefull into your water
it will be the better.

Mr. Triplett's Receipt for the Ague.

Take 3 Gallons of Aqua-vitæ, put into
it halfe a bushell of red poppy flowers,
lett it stand a day and a night in
a glass well stopt[;] then straine it

. . . .

40

very well, and put in it the same glass
againe[;] take halfe a pound of figgs,
halfe a pound of raisons of the sunn,
well stoned, and sliced, 3 ounces of
Anniseeds beate small[;] tye all
these in a bagg, lett it stand upon
these ingredients[;] if you have a
Convenient place to sun it for 10
days, it will much improve it.

Note: Be sure the poppy lie not in the
Aqua-vitfl above 24. houres.
In 2. or 3. sponefulls of this water
dissolve well the quantity of an
hasel nutt of London Treakle[;] give
it the patient an hour before
the fitt fasting, then exercise
a fast 4. or 5. hours after.

A white ffrigasy.

Take the fleash of 6 Chickens, &
cut the leggs and wings into peeces,
and the other cutt in as broad thin
peeces as you cann[;] then take strong
broth, and a bundle of sweet herbs,
and large mace, and boyle all

. . . .

41

together till they be tender[;] then put
your Chickens into the pan, then

take 9 yelkes of Eggs, and beate
them with a litle white wine,
or a little Vinigar, a little sugar,
and the Iuice of a limon, but fry
your Chickens[;] when they are
ready then put in your Eggs, and
toss them well together, fry them
not too long after your Eggs be in,
for they will Curdle[;] soe serve yᵐ
with Cippits[;] straw minced parcly
over the Dish.

To make a limon Sallett.

Take limons, and cut them in yᵉ midst
and take out the meate, and put them
into a Bason of cold water, then lett
them stand all night in cold water,
and the next morning cut them out
into little long strings, and wind them
up every halfe limon by it selfe, and
tye them with a thread, that they
doe not breake[;] then take them, &
boyle them till they be a little tender[;] then take a pint of Vinigar

. . . .

42

and a pound of sugar, and boyle yᵐ
till they come to a thicke Sirrope.

How to make an Excellent fine Cake

Take a quarter of a Peck, or some-what
more, of the finest flower you can gett,
a pint of thicke Creame, 10 yelkes, (with
out whites) well beaten, 3 quarters of a
pound of fresh butter gently melted, and
poured on the flower, a little dish full
of Aile yeast strained, halfe a quarter
of a pint of Rosewater, with some musk
or Amber-greece dissolved in it[;] season

it with salt, a penny-worth of Cloves,
and as much mace, and more of Nutmegge, all finely beaten together,
2 pound of the best Currence, well pickt,
and washed in warme water, a pound
of raisons stoned, and shred very small,
with a little rose-water, halfe a pound of
fine sugar, first mingled, then knead, all
these things very well together, then
lett them lye a full hour in their dough,

. . . .

43

and the Oven being ready make up
your Cake; lett not your oven be too
hott, shutt not the mouth of it close,
turne your Cake now, and then[,] that
it may bake alike; lett it not stand a
full hour in the Oven, against the
time you draw your Cake; you must
have in readynes some Rosewater,
and sugar beaten small, and both
together beaten in a pottenger[;] then
dip in a tuffe of feathers, or a little
brush in it, and wet the upper side of
the Cake all over very well, then
sett your Cake in the Oven, to dry
it on, and when you draw your Cake
it will be covered as it were with Gee;
Note: This is called Queene Elizabeth's fine
Cake.

To stew a Rump of Beefe.

Take a Rump of Beefe, and cut it
into 4. peeces, put it into a great
pipkin with water[;] cut 4. or 5. Carrotts
in peeces, put good store of Onyons shred,
3 leaves of mace, and some whole

. . . .

44

pepper, a bundle of time, and Rose-

mary, 6 sponefulls of Vinigar, a
pint and halfe of Renish wine,
a little verjuice, and salt[;] lett it
stand a great while softly, and
then send it in with browne Cippits.

A white-Pott.

To a quart of Creame, take 8 yelks
of Eggs, the whites of 2, beate y^{m}
very well, season them with sugar,
rose-water, nutmegge, 4. dates sliced[;]
take a peny lofe and slice it thin, then
put it into a dish, with the marrow
of 2 bones, butter the bottome of the
dish, and strew the raisons at top[;]
an hour will bake it.

To make a good Posset.

Take 8 yelkes of Eggs, and whites, beate
them well together, and straine y^{m}
into a quart of Creame, season them
with nutmeggs, and put to them a pint
of sack, stir them together, and put

. . . .

45

them into a bason, and sett it into
an Oven noe hotter then for Custards[;]
lett them stand in 2 hours.

To make an Excellent Sillibubbe.

Fill your Sillibubbe pot with Sider,
and good store of sugar, and a little
Nutmegge, stir it well together,
and when the Sugar is melted, put
in as much creame, by 2. or 3. sponefulls at a time[;] then stirre it softly
once about, lett it stand 2 hours at
least before it be eaten[;] the standing
makes it curdle.

To make Gumballs

To a pound of fine flower dryed in
the Oven take a quarter of a pound
of sugar, 2 yelks of Eggs, and one
white, and thicke creame as
much as will wett it, Corriander[,]
fennell seed a good quantity[;] worke
all together well, then roll it into
small rolls, and cast it into Knotts[;]
Take heed the Oven be not too hott.

. . . .

A sirrope for a Cough   46
of the Lungs. by D. R.

Take a good deale of wood-Bittony, Sca-
bias, Egrimony, Colesfoot, Senecle,
ale hoofe, tub a like quantity of
these hearbs, (except alesfoote)[;]
take a little less of this, because it
is of a strong tast[;] beate these in a
stone morter, and wring out the
Guice a pint, or a quart (as you
will)[;] then sett it on the fire, and
skim it just as it boyleth, that it
may be cleared[;] then to a pound
of hony lett there be a pound and
a quarter of the iuice, and put
them altogether, and boyle them
to a Sirrope, and take a Sponefull
or 2 of this Sirrope, morning and
Evening.

. . . .

47 **To preserve Damaske roses**

Take Damaske-Rosebudds, with the
nailes upon them, and shake y^e
seeds from them, halfe a peck, pick

them cleane from the outleaves, put
to them as much runing water as
will cover them[;] when they are thrust
downe, and prest altogether, boyle them
till they be tender close covered[;] put
in double the weight, and halfe of
fine sugar, and boyle them to a
Conserve[;] your sugar must be put in
at twice from the time you put in
your first sugar, till it be enough it
will be an hour, but lett it not be too
long after your last sugar in[;] you
must not cover it after you begin
to put in your sugar.
    Take a sponefull of it at a time,
(doe more as you will have it worke)
in a morning early, and keepe in
a warme house, but you may goe
about ye house if you will.

. . . .

To preserve Raspas.   48

Take a quart of Raspas, and put
them into a Skillet, and boyle y^m
a little, untill the juice will come
from them, then straine them
through a peece of Canvas, then
take a pound and a quarter of lofe
sugar well beaten, and put to the
sugar halfe a pint of the Iuice of
the Raspas, and sett it on a quick
fire, and boyle it and skim it[;] then
boyle that liquor till it come to a
thick sirrope[;] then take it of[f] from
the fire, skim it cleane, and put
in a pound of great Raspas, and
lett them stand in the liquor a
little while till they are warme[;]
then set them on the fire, and
boyle them a little while gently[;]
then boyle them on a quick fire,
and soe boyle them till they be e-
nough, which will be quickly, but if
you boyle them long they will be hard.

The Index.

Preserves, & Conserves.

· ·

The Index.

Cokery.

· ·

Phisike & Chirurgery.
Index.

· ·

I. I.

THE
QUEENE-LIKE CLOSET
Or
RICH CABINET

Printed for Rich: Lownes
at the white Lion in Duck Layne neare West smith field 1675

The Queen=like Closet,

OR

RICH CABINET:

Stored with all manner of

RARE RECEIPTS

FOR

Preserving, Candying and Cookery.

Very Pleasant and Beneficial to all
Ingenious Persons of the FEMALE SEX.

To which is added,

A SUPPLEMENT,

PRESENTED

To all Ingenious LADIES,
and GENTLEWOMEN.

By *Hannah Wolley.*

The Third EDITION.

LONDON,
Printed for *Richard Lowndes* at the *White
Lion* in *Duck-Lane,* near *West-
Smithfield,* 1675.

APPENDIX II: "TO SERVE IN NOBLE OR GREAT HOUSES"

from Hannah Woolley,
The Queen-like Closet (London, 1675)

Hannah Woolley instructed her audiences about hospitality and servitude after the Civil War for "the general good of my country." Her manual illustrates the fluctuations in the social order as well as the growing attention given to private dining and entertaining. As servants to noble families, children and young adults acquired important skills for their own future households. Women are more visible in the household workings and "even Gentlewomen [are] forced to serve." Conversely, a cook-maid may become Mistress of a household herself. For young cook-maids exposed to noble methods of flavoring, cooking, and serving dishes, their "good memory" became the basis of their own home cookery. Woolley writes that she is "blamed by many for divulging these Secrets, and again commended by others for my Love and Charity in so doing."

Now because I would have every one Complete who have a Desire to serve in Noble or Great Houses, I shall here shew them what their Office requires; And,

First, For the Kitchin, because without that we shall look lean, and grow faint quickly.

The Cook, whether Man or Woman, ought to be very well skill'd in all manner of things both Fish and Flesh, also good at Pastry business, seasoning of all things, and knowing all kinds of Sauces, and pickling all manner of Pickles, in making all manner of Meat Jellies; also very frugal of their Lords or of their Masters, Ladies or Mistresses Purse, very saving, cleanly and careful, obliging to all persons, kind to those under them, and willing to inform them, quiet in their Office, not swearing nor cursing, nor wrangling, but silently and ingeniously to do their Business, and neat and quick about it; they ought also to have a very good Fancy: such an one, whether Man or Woman, deserves the title of a fit Cook.

For a Maid under such a Cook

She ought to be of a quick and nimble Apprehension, neat and cleanly in her own habit, and then we need not doubt of it in her Office; not to dress her self, specially her head, in the Kitchin, for that is abominable sluttish, but in her Chamber before she comes down, and that to be at a fit hour, that the fire may be made, and all things prepared for the Cook, against he or she comes in; she must not have a sharp Tongue, but humble, pleasing, and willing to learn; for ill words may provoke Blows from a Cook, their heads being always filled with the contrivance of their business, which may cause them to be peevish and froward, if provoked to it; this Maid ought also to have a good Memory, and not to forget from one day to another what should be done, nor to leave any manner of thing foul at night, neither in the

Kitchin, nor Larders, to keep her Iron things and others clean scowred, and the Floors clean as well as places above them; not to sit up junketting and gigling with Fellows, when she should be in Bed, such an one is a Consumer of her Masters Goods, and no better than a Thief; and besides, such Behaviour savoureth much of Levity. But such an one that will take the Counsel I have seriously given, will not only make her Superiours happy in a good Servant, but she will make her self happy also; for by her Industry she may come one day to be Mistress over others.

Now to the Butler

He ought to be Gentile and Neat in his Habit, and in his Behaviour, courteous to all people, yet very saving of his Masters Goods, and to order himself in his Office as a faithful Steward, charge and do all things for the honour of his Master or Lady, not suffering their Wine or Strong Drink to be devoured by ill Companies, nor the Small to be drawn out in waste, nor Pieces of good Bread to lie to mould and spoil; he must keep his Vessels close stopped, and his Bottles sweet, his Cellars clean washed, and his Buttery clean, and his Bread-Bins wholsome and sweet, his Knives whetted, his Glasses clean washed, that there be no dimness upon them, when they come to be used, all his Plate clean and bright, his Table, Basket and Linnen very neat, he must be sure to have all things of Sauce ready which is for him to bring forth, that it may not be to be fetched when it is call'd for, as Oyl, Vinegar, Sugar, Salt, Mustard, Oranges and Limons, and also some Pepper; he must also be very neat and handy in laying the Clothes for the Chief Table, and also the Side-boards, in laying his Napkins in several Fashions, and pleiting them, to set his Glasses, Plate, and Trencher-Plates in order upon the Side-Boards, his Water-Glasses, Oranges or Limons; that he be careful to set the Salts on the Table, and to lay a Knife, Spoon and Fork at every Plate, that his Bread be chipped before he brings it in; that he set Drink to warm in due time if the season require; that he observes a fit time to set Chairs or Stools, that he have his Cistern ready to set his Drink in; that none be spilt about the Room, to wash the Glasses when any one hath drunk, and to wait diligently on them at the Table, not filling the Glasses too full; such an one may call himself a Butler.

To the Carver

If any Gentleman who attends the Table, be employed or commanded to cut up any Fowl or Pig, or any thing else whatsoever, it is requisite that he have a clean Napkin upon his Arm, and a Knife and Fork for his use; that he take that dish he should Carve, from the Table till he hath made it ready for his Superiours to eat, and neatly and handsomly to carve it, not touching of it so near as he can with his Fingers, but if he chance unawares to do so, not to lick his Fingers, but wipe them upon a Cloth, or his Napkin, which he hath for that purpose; for otherwise it is unhandsome and unmannerly; the neatest Carvers never touch any Meat but with the Knife and Fork; he must be very nimble lest the Meat cool to much, and when he hath done, return it to the Table again, putting away his Carving Napkin, and take a clean one to wait withal; he must be very Gentile and Gallant in his Habit, lest he be deemed unfit to attend such Persons.

To all other Men-Servants or Maid-Servants who commonly attend such Tables.

They must all be neat and cleanly in their Habit, and keep their Heads clean kembed, always ready at the least Call and very attentive to hear any one at the Table, to set Chairs or Stools, and not to give any a foul Napkin, but see that every one whom their Lord or Master is pleased to admit to their Table, have every thing which is fit for them, and that they change their Plates when need shall be; also that they observe the eyes of a Stranger what they want, and not force them still to want because they are silent, because it is not very modest for an Inferious to speak aloud before their Betters; and it is more unfit they should want, since they have leave to eat and drink: they must wait diligently, and at a distance from the Table, not daring to lean on the Chairs for soiling them, or shewing Rudeness; for to lean on a Chair when they wait, is a particular favour shewn to any superious Servant, as the Chief Gentleman, or the Waiting Woman when she rises from the Table; they must not hold the Plates before their Mouths to be defiled with their Breath, nor touch them on the right side; when the Lord, Master, Lady or Mistress shew that favour to drink to any Inferiour, and do command them to fill for them to pledge them, it is not modesty for them to deny

Strangers that favour, as commonly they do, but to fulfill their Commands, or else they dishonour the Favour.

When any Dish is taken off the Table, they must not set it down for Dogs to eat, nor eat it themselves by the way, but haste into the Kitchin with it to the Cook, that he may see what is to be set away, and what to be kept hot for Servants; when all is taken away, and Thanks given, they must help the Butler out with those things which belong to him, that he may not lose his Dinner.

They must be careful also to lay the Cloth for themselves, and see that nothing be wanting at the Table, and to call the rest of the Servants to Meals, whose Office was not to wait at the Table, then to sit down in a handsome manner, and to be courteous to every Stranger, especially the Servants of those Persons whom their Lord or Master hath a kindness for.

If any poor Body comes to ask an Alms, do not shut the Door against them rudely, but be modest and civil to them, and see if you can procure somewhat for them, and think with yourselves, that though you are now full fed, and well cloathed, and free from care, yet you know not what may be your condition another day: So much to Inferiour Servants.

To the Gentlewomen who have the Charge of the Sweet-Meats, and such like Repasts.

   Gentlewomen,

Perhaps you do already know what belongs to serving in fine Cream Cheeses, Jellies, Leaches or Sweet-meats, or to set forth Banquets as well as I do; but (pardon me) I speak not to any knowing Person, but to the Ignorant, because they may not remain so; besides really there are new Modes come up now adays for eating and drinking, as well as for Clothes, and the most knowing of you all may perhaps find somewhat here which you have not already seen; and for the Ignorant, I am sure they may ground themselves very well from hence in many accomplishments, and truly I have taken this pains to impart these things for the general good of my Country, as well as my own, and have done it with the more willingness, since I find so many Gentlewomen forced to serve, whose Parents and Friends have been impoverished by the late Calamities, *viz.* the late Wars, Plague, and Fire, and to see what mean Places they are forced to be in, because they want Accomplishments for better.

I am blamed by many for divulging these Secrets, and again commended by others for my Love and Charity in so doing; but however I am better satisfied with imparting them, than to let them die with me; and if I do not live to have the comfort of your thanks, yet I hope it will cause you to speak well of me when I am dead: The Books which before this I have caused to be put in Print, found so good an acceptance, as that I shall still go on in imparting what I yet have so fast as I can.

Now to begin with the Ordering those things named to you:

If it be but a private Dinner or Supper in a Noble House, where they have none to honour above themselves, I presume it may be thus:

In Summer time, when the Meat is all taken away, you may present your several sorts of Cream Cheeses; One Meal one Dish of Cream of one sort, the next of another; one or two Scollop Dishes with several sorts of Fruit, which if it be small Fruit, as Rasps or Strawberries, they must be first washed in Wine in a Dish or Bason, and taken up between two Spoons, that you touch them not.

With them you may serve three or four small dishes also with Sweet-meats, such as are most in season, with Vine Leaves and Flowers between the Dishes and the Plates, two wet Sweet-meats, and two dry, two of one colour, and two of another, or all of several colours.

Also a Dish of Jellies of several colours in one Dish, if such be required.

If any be left, you may melt them again, and put them into lesser Glasses, and they will be for another time:

If any dry ones be left, they are soon put into the Boxes again.

If any persons come in the Afternoon, if no greater, or so great as the Person who entertains them, then you may present one or two Dishes of Cream only, and a whipt Sillibub, or other, with about four Dishes of Sweet-meats served in, in like manner as at Dinner, with dishes of Fruit, and some kind of Wine of your own making; at Evenings, especially on Fasting Days at Night, it is fit to present some pretty kind of Cream, contrary from those at Dinner, or instead of them some Possets, or other fine Spoon

Meats, which may be pleasant to the taste, with some wet and dry Sweet-meats and some of your fine Drinks, what may be most pleasing.

At a Feast, you may present these things following.

So soon as the Meat is quite taken away, have in readiness your Cream Cheeses of several sorts and of several Colours upon a Salver, then some fresh Cheese with Wine and Sugar, another Dish of Clouted Cream, and a Noch with Cabbage Cream of several Colours like a Cabbage; then all sorts of Fruits in season, set forth as followeth:

First You must have a large Salver made of light kind of Wood, that it may not be too heavy for the Servitor to carry, it must be painted over, and large enough to hold six Plates round about and one larger one in the middle, there must be places made in it to set the Plates in, that they may be very fast and sure from sliding, and that in the middle the seat must be much higher than all the rest, because that is most gracefull; your Plates must not be so broad as the Trencher Plates at Meat, and should be either of Silver or China.

Set your Plates fast, then fill every one with several sorts of Fruits, and the biggest sort in the middle, you must lay them in very good order, and pile them up till one more will not lie; then stick them with little green Sprigs and fine Flowers, such as you fancy best; then serve in another such Salver, with Plates piled up with all manner of Sweet-meats, the wet sweet-meats round about and the dry in the middle, your wet Sweet-meats must be in little glasses that you may set the more on, and between every two glasses another above the first of all, and one on the top of them all; you must put of all sorts of dryed Sweet-meats in the middle Plate, first your biggest and then your lesser, till you can lay no more; then stick them all with Flowers and serve them: And in the Bason of Water you send in to wash the Hands or Fingers of Noble Persons, you must put in some Orange Flower Water, which is very rare and very pleasant.

In Winter you must alter, as to the season, but serve all in this manner; and then dryed Fruits will also be very acceptable; as dryed Pears and Pippins, Candied Oranges and Limons, Citrons and Eringoes, Blanched Almonds, Prunels, Figs, Raisins, Pistachoes, and Blanched Walnuts.

FINIS

GLOSSARY

Agrimony (also, **Egrimony**) - a popular, domestic medicinal herb whose dried leaves were often brewed as a "spring drink" or "diet drink" to purify the blood

Ambergris (also, **Ambergrease**) - a wax-like substance found floating in tropical seas and as a secretion in the intestines of the sperm whale; it is odiferous and is used in perfumery, formerly in cookery

Aqua vitae - a term of the alchemists; applied to ardent spirits or unrectified alcohol; sometimes applied to ardent spirits of the first distillation

Bombust (also, **Bombast**) - the soft down of the cotton plant, raw cotton, or cotton wool

Chadarne (also, **Chawdron**) - entrails; also a kind of sauce consisting of chopped entrails, spices, and other ingredients

Cheeks - as a cut of meat, the jawbone, the chaps, chops, or fauces; the swallow, or gullet

Chiny (also, **Chynie**) - the whole or part of the backbone of an animal, with the adjoining flesh

Clary - a sweet liquor consisting of a mixture of wine, clarified honey, and various spices such as pepper and ginger; also a variety of Sage often added to ale and beer to make it more heady

Decoction - a liquor in which a substance has been boiled so its principles are extracted and dissolved; specifically, as a medicinal agent

Dragon - the plant *Dracunculus,* known as Dragons, or Dragonwort; also applied to the species *Dracontium*; also a corruption of Dragant, as in Gum dragon, or Tragacanth

Ember weeks - the name applied to four periods of fasting and prayer appointed by the Church to be observed respectively in the four seasons of the year

Fool (also, **Foole**) - a dish composed of fruit that has been stewed, crushed, and mixed with milk, cream, or custard; often gooseberry fool

Fricassee (also, **Frigasy**) - a dish of meat that has been sautéed or fried before being stewed with vegetables; a thick, chunky stew

Gee (also, **Ghee**) - butter made from buffalo's milk, clarified by boiling so it will resemble oil in consistency

Graine - the smallest English unit of weight, now 1/5760 of a lb., but originally a grain of corn or wheat, dry; the smallest possible quantity

Humors (also, **Humours**) - the four chief fluids of the body (blood, phlegm, choler, melancholy) whose relative proportions determine a person's physical and mental qualities and disposition

Liaison - a thickening for sauces, chiefly the yolks of eggs; also the process of thickening

Marchpane (also, **Marzipan**) - a confection composed of the paste of pounded almonds, sugar, etc., made up into small cakes or molded into decorative shapes

Mastick (also, **Mastic**) - a gum or resin exuded from the bark of *Pistacia Lentiscus,* formerly much used in medicine; also Herb Mastic, the plant *Thymus Mastichina*

Megrim (also, **Migraine**) - a from of severe headache

Muscadine - a thick-skinned purple grape with a strong, musky flavor or odor; also muscadine-wine, or muscatel

Pennyroyal - a species of mint with small leaves and prostrate habit, esteemed for its supposed medicinal virtues

Physick (also, **Physic**) - a cathartic or purge; a curative regimen

Pottle - a little pot, or, a measure; a liquid measure equal to two quarts, or half a gallon; a pot or vessel containing a pottle

Purslane - a low, succulent herb used in salads, and sometimes as a pot-herb, or for pickling

Raines (also, **Reins**) - the kidneys; also the region of the kidneys; the loins

Rennet (also, **Runnett**) - a preparation used to curdle milk; often the plant known as Lady's Bedstraw; also, a mass of curdled milk found in the stomach of an unweaned calf or other animal, used for curdling milk in the making of cheese, or a preparation of the inner membrane of the stomach used for the same purpose; also the name of a class of dessert apples of French origin

Rocket - a kind of cabbage often used in salads; also wild rocket, or hedge mustard

Sack - a general name for a class of white wines formerly imported from Spain and the Canaries

Searched (also, **Searced, Sieved**) - sifted

Simple - a medicinal preparation composed or concocted of only one ingredient, especially of one herb or plant; also, a plant or herb employed for medicinal purposes

Snow - a dish or confection that resembles snow in appearance; often made by whipping the white of eggs to a creamy consistency

Still-room - originally, a room in a house in which a still was kept for the distillation of perfumes and cordials; later, a room where preserves, cakes, liqueurs, etc., were kept and where tea, coffee, etc., were prepared

Verven (also, **Vervain**) - the common European and British herbaceous plant, *verbena officinalis*, formerly much valued for its reputed medicinal properties

Water - an aqueous decoction, infusion, or tincture, used medicinally or as a cosmetic or perfume

Alley, Hugh. *Hugh Alley's Caveat: the markets of London in 1598.* Folger Ms. V.a.318. Edited by Ian Archer, Caroline Barron, and Vanessa Harding. London: London Topographical Society, 1988.

Ambrosoli, Mauro. *The wild and the sown: botany and agriculture in western Europe, 1350–1850.* Translated by Mary McCann Salvatorelli. Cambridge: Cambridge University Press, 1997.

Appleby, Andrew. "Diet in sixteenth-century England: sources, problems, possibilities." In *Health, medicine, and mortality in the sixteenth century.* Edited by Charles Webster. Cambridge: Cambridge University Press, 1979.

Archer, Michael. *Delftware: the tin-glazed earthenware of the British Isles.* London: Victoria & Albert Museum, 1997.

Bennett, H. S. *English books and readers, 1475–1557.* 2nd ed. Cambridge: Cambridge University Press, 1969.

Best, Michael R., see Markham, Gervase.

Brown, Peter B. *In praise of hot liquors: the study of chocolate, coffee, and tea-drinking, 1600–1850.* York, England: York Civic Trust, 1995.

Chappell, William. *Popular music of the olden time; a collection of ancient songs, ballads, and dance tunes.* London: Cramer, Beale, & Chappell, [1859].

Chartres, John, and David Hey, eds. *English rural society, 1500–1800: essays in honour of Joan Thirsk.* Cambridge: Cambridge University Press, 1990.

Cressy, David. *Literacy and the social order: reading and writing in Tudor and Stuart England.* Cambridge: Cambridge University Press, 1980.

Darell, Walter. *A short discourse of the life of serving-men.* London: For Ralph Newberrie, 1578.

Davidson, Caroline. *The Ham House kitchen.* London: Victoria & Albert Museum, 1993.

Doggett, Rachel, ed. *New world of wonders: European images of the Americas, 1492–1700.* Washington, D.C.: The Folger Shakespeare Library, 1992.

Evelyn, John. *Acetaria: a discourse of sallets* (1699). Edited by Christopher Driver. Devon, England: Prospect Books, 1996.

Everitt, Alan. "The market towns." In *The early modern town: a reader.* Edited by Peter Clark. London: Longman, 1976.

Fettiplace, Elinor. *Elinor Fettiplace's receipt book: Elizabethan country house cooking.* Hilary Spurling, editor. London: Viking Salamander, 1986.

Fischer, David Hackett. *Albion's seed: four British folkways in America.* New York: Oxford University Press, 1989.

Gentil, François. *Le jardinier solitaire. The solitary or Carthusian gard'ner.* London: B. Tooke, 1706.

Gerard, John. *The herbal: or, general history of plants.* New York: Dover Publications, 1975.

Gerard, John. *Leaves from Gerard's herball.* Edited by Marcus Woodward. New York: Dover Publications, 1969.

Grigsby, Leslie, with Michael Archer, Margaret Macfarlane, and Jonathan Horne. *The Longridge collection of English slipware and delftware.* London: Jonathan Horne, forthcoming.

Harrison, William. *The description of England: the classic contemporary account of Tudor social life.* Edited by Georges Edelen. Washington, D.C., & New York: The Folger Shakespeare Library and Dover Publications, 1994.

Hartley, Dorothy. *Lost country life.* New York: Pantheon Books, 1979.

Hess, Karen, see *Martha Washington's Booke.*

Hoby, Lady Margaret. *Diary . . . , 1599–1605.* Edited by Dorothy M. Meads. London: Routledge, 1930.

Holme, Randle. *The academy of armory.* London: Roxburghe Club, 1905.

Hull, Suzanne. *Chaste, silent, and obedient: English books for women, 1475–1640.* San Marino: Huntington Library, 1982.

Hume, Audrey Noel. *Archaeology and the colonial gardener.* Williamsburg: Colonial Williamsburg Foundation, 1974.

Kerridge, Eric. *The agricultural revolution.* New York: A. M. Kelley, 1968.

Kiefer, Frederick. *Writing on the Renaissance stage: written words, printed pages, metaphoric books.* Newark: University of Delaware Press; London: Associated University Presses, 1996.

Marcoux, Paula. "The thickening plot: notable liaisons between French and English cookbooks, 1600–1660." *Petits Propos Culinaires,* 60 (December 1998), 8–20.

Markham, Gervase. *Countrey contentments, in two bookes . . . the second intituled, the English huswife.* London, 1605.

Markham, Gervase. *The English housewife.* Edited by Michael R. Best. Kingston: McGill-Queen's University Press, c1986.

Martha Washington's Booke of cookery and Booke of sweetmeats. Transcribed by Karen Hess. New York: Columbia University Press, 1995.

May, Robert. *The accomplisht cook.* Edited by Alan Davidson, Marcus Bell, and Tom Jaine. Totnes, England: Prospect Books, 1997.

Mendelson, Sara Heller, and Patricia Crawford. *Women in early modern England, 1550–1720*. Oxford: Clarendon Press, 1998.

Nissenbaum, Stephen. *The battle for Christmas*. New York: Vintage Books, 1997.

Orlin, Lena Cowen. *Elizabethan households: an anthology*. Washington, D.C.: The Folger Shakespeare Library, 1995.

Palliser, D. M. *The age of Elizabeth: England under the later Tudors, 1547–1603*. Second ed. London: Longman, 1992.

Paston-Williams, Sarah. *The art of dining*. London: The National Trust, 1993.

Rohde, Eleanour Sinclair. *The old English herbals*. New York: Dover Publications, 1970.

Sanders, Eve Rachele. *Gender and literacy on stage in early modern England*. Cambridge: Cambridge University Press, 1998.

Spufford, Margaret. *Small books and pleasant histories: popular fiction and its readership in seventeenth-century England*. Cambridge: Cambridge University Press, 1980.

Spurling, Hilary, see Fettiplace, Elinor.

Stow, John. *A survey of the cities of London and Westminster and the borough of Southwark*. London, 1754–1755.

Thick, Malcolm. *The neat house gardens: early market gardening around London*. Totnes, England: Prospect Books, 1998.

Thick, Malcolm. "Root crops and the feeding of London's poor in the late 16th and 17th centuries." In Chartres, John, and David Hey, eds. *English rural society, 1500–1800*. Cambridge: Cambridge University Press, 1990.

Thirsk, Joan. *Economic policy and projects: the development of a consumer society in early modern England*. Oxford: Clarendon Press, 1978.

Thomas, Keith. *Man and the natural world: changing attitudes in England, 1500–1800*. Oxford: Oxford University Press, 1996.

Thomas, Keith. "The meaning of literacy in early modern England." In *The written word: literacy in transition*. Edited by Gerd Baumann. Oxford: Clarendon Press, 1986.

Trager, James. *The food chronology*. New York: Henry Holt, 1995.

Tusser, Thomas. *A hundreth good pointes of husbandrie*. London: R. Tottel, 1557.

Vives, Juan Luis. *Tudor school-boy life: the dialogues of Juan Luis Vives*. Translated…into English…by Foster Watson. London: J. M. Dent & Co., 1908.

Wheaton, Barbara Ketchum. *Savoring the past: the French kitchen and table from 1300 to 1789*. Philadelphia: University of Pennsylvania Press, 1983.

Williams, Neville. *The maritime trade of the East Anglian ports, 1550–1590*. Oxford: Clarendon Press, 1988.

Wilson, C. Anne, ed. *"Banquetting stuffe": the fare and social background of the Tudor and Stuart banquet*. Leeds Symposium on Food History and Traditions, 1986. Edinburgh: Edinburgh University Press, 1990.

Wilson, C. Anne. *Food and drink in Britain from the Stone Age to recent times*. London: Constable, 1973.

Woodward, Donald. "'An essay on manures': changing attitudes to fertilization in England, 1500–1800." In Chartres, John, and David Hey, eds. *English rural society, 1500–1800*. Cambridge: Cambridge University Press, 1990.

Wrightson, Keith. *English society, 1580–1680*. New Brunswick: Rutgers University Press, 1982.